DIVORCE AND REMARRIAGE IN THE CHURCH

DIVORCE AND REMARRIAGE IN THE CHURCH

Stanley A. Ellisen

Lamplighter Books
Grand Rapids, Michigan
Zondervan Publishing House

Divorce and Remarriage in the Church

© 1977, 1980 by The Zondervan Corporation
Grand Rapids, Michigan

Lamplighter Books are published by Zondervan Publishing House,
1415 Lake Drive, S.E., Grand Rapids, Michigan 49506

Library of Congress Cataloging in Publication Data
Ellisen, Stanley A
    Divorce and remarriage in the church.

    1. Divorce.   2. Remarriage.   I. Title
BT707.E47   261.8'34'2   77-9945

ISBN 0-310-35561-3

Printed in the United States of America

87 88 89 90 / 15 14 13 12 11 10

To my wife, EVELYN
God's gift and "complement"
for nearly twenty-five years

Contents

Introduction

The most valuable things in life are often the most vulnerable. Ironically, it's dangerous to be dear. That is certainly true of the marriage relationship which is under brutal attack in our time. To guard against that vulnerability, however, the Lord has provided the Christian couple a protective shield of biblical principles. The pity is that these principles are not clearly understood by all.

These pages then are for all Christian couples, not just for those facing marriage difficulties. Although the Lord's counsel on divorce and remarriage will be highlighted as the "pound of cure," these principles will be introduced by an emphasis on His "ounce of prevention." Only by a proper understanding of God's purpose in marriage can the difficulties and solution to marriage breakup be understood.

Having outlined and taught through the Bible many times, I am convinced that the Bible is clear and consistent in its matrimonial principles. The Bible writers do not contradict themselves, but give us an amazingly consistent set of simple guidelines to follow. As the plan of salvation should be second nature to every believer, so the principles for achieving marital harmony and happiness should be understood by all. Let's spend a couple hours at the office of God, the wonderful marriage Counselor, and review His principles for achieving marital happiness. His counsel could be life-changing.

DIVORCE
AND
REMARRIAGE
IN THE
CHURCH

1
The Marriage Relation: Where Angels Fear to Tread

In response to the question as to why married men live longer than single men, the wag replied, "They don't live longer; it just seems longer." His wry humor actually revealed the sentiment of many today toward marriage. It's a great institution, they feel, but "who wants to be in an institution?"

Let's face it. The modern home is in trouble, serious trouble. A souring process has set in. Created as God's magnum opus and commanded not to be destroyed, it appears to be falling apart at the seams, especially the central seam of the marriage relation. Divorce has practically become a way of life in our society. It is more and more regarded as a handy escape hatch when marriage difficulties arise to frustrate the relationship.

Some Alarming Statistics

To bring the immensity of the problem into sharper focus, we might recall a few recent figures from the Vital Statistics Bureau. There were 1,050,000 divorces in the U.S.A. in 1975, an increase of 16% over 1974. For the first quarter of 1976, the State of Washington reported that legal divorces there were nearly equal to the number of marriages (actually 6630 to 7214). This was an increase of

13

6.5% in divorces over the previous year. In 1975, the State of Oregon reported 15,750 divorces to 17,510 marriages, an increase of 16% in one year. Marriages declined during the same year 12.5% (perhaps reflecting the increasing live-in situations). The national marriage-divorce ratio, according to the National Center for Health Statistics, is currently listed as 3 to 2. A strange "liberty" seems to have been proclaimed throughout the land.

In addition to this increase in legal divorces, another type of separation has become popular and should be noted to get the full picture. Andre Bustanoby, a marriage counselor and researcher from Bowie, Maryland, has noted that desertions (called a "poor man's divorce") almost equal the number of legal divorces. This suggests that divorces and separations already are outnumbering marriages today. These figures, however, do not include the countless common-law arrangements and breakups which have increased in our age among both the young and old. It should be noted furthermore that many continuing marriages actually are unions in name and address only. Numerous such marriages are continued for convenience, because of social pressure, or for the sake of the children. If these discontents had their "druthers" the divorce statistics would explode.

This phenomena of increasing marriage dissolutions apparently is being taken in quiet stride by our generation. Though its prevalence is alarming, its increasing acceptability is even more so. Little national hand-wringing is noticeable. The marriage vows for many are a tongue-in-cheek recital, with the tacit understanding, "till divorce do us part." Even some churches are thinking in terms of dignifying divorce with a church ceremony. The sting is being taken out so that when the zig-zags get out of rhythm, the avenue of divorce is a perfectly legitimate option.

This "release me and let me love again" syndrome is not confined to the Hollywood or Broadway set, but reaches into all segments of our society. Its incidence is seen in the backgrounds of a recent president and vice-president, as well as in the lives of numerous congressmen. Though divorce until recently was an impossible handicap for one running for high office, the subject today hardly raises an eyebrow. Its cultural acceptability is barely questioned. And lest we as a church become judgmental and self-righteous in this regard, we need to recall that countless pastors also have fallen victim to this marital tragedy. It pervades our society. One prominent pastor recently said that he had "presided over" more divorces than marriages in his last parish. In our community I was reminded how close to home the problem is when I reflected that within a few houses of ours, three families have suffered marriage breakups within the last two years. With only one marriage in that time, the ratio amounts to an inverted 3 to 1 for our neighborhood.

This increasing acceptability of divorce in recent years, of course, has given it further impetus. It is almost indecent to question its respectability. In our permissive age of doing what comes naturally, we have adopted the principle of realism and forthrightness in reaction to anything that smacks of hypocrisy. It is more "religious" today to be realistic and "fulfilled" (whatever that is), than to be idealistic and "tough it out." Thus our permissive attitude has promoted our acceptance of divorce, and the two tend to outrun each other. There is certainly no sign of a turn-about, if the hard statistics are any indication.

The Church's Responsibility

These marital statistics have not been cited to alarm, but to alert. The problem is not theirs, but ours. It is ours

15

because we have the remedy and the principles for the prevention of marital dissolution. It is ours because we are our "brother's keeper," and their lives inevitably affect ours. We cannot condemn and cast stones for they will assuredly turn into boomerangs on our own glass houses and rebuke us in our progeny. We need to quit piously kidding ourselves and skirting the issue. Every believer has a responsibility to understand the problem and its biblical solution, for we all will sooner or later be faced with the problem in our churches or in other relationships.

We would therefore underscore the fact that this discussion on marital problems is not designed merely for those personally involved or the delinquent. It is pertinent for all believers who desire to be conversant with the biblical data and God's will on this most foundational issue. So deep and broad is the problem that God has a special word for each of us on the subject. For those entering the marriage arena or already enjoying a happy marriage, God has some words of clarification and caution. For those whose marriage is shaky or faltering, God has a preventive solution that must be understood in terms of long-range principles. For those who have succumbed to the tragedy of divorce, it is necessary to know God's way back. He has not deserted you in your marriage shipwreck, but is anxious to counsel and guide. Where divorce and remarriage have already taken place, God also has a definite word of counsel and clarification for restoration. He has redemptive counsel for all. But the principles He has laid down for such situations must be assimilated and acted upon to enable a life of peace and productivity in Christian living. Every believer is responsible to know these biblical principles.

Furthermore, the church itself has a grave and far-reaching responsibility in this regard. Ironically, there are few issues on which the church is so confused and uncertain as on the problem of divorce and remarriage. Small wonder, since so many pastors also share that confusion. Some pastors will marry divorced people; some will marry some, but not others; and yet others will not pronounce a pastoral blessing on any second-go-round of marriage apart from the death of one of the partners. With that confusion, what is a church member to do or believe on the subject? Our stammering tongue on the subject only engenders a spirit of either legalistic dogmatism or realistic permissivism. With so many positions taken on the issue, we hardly know how to view those in the church with a history of divorce or where to allow them to serve the Lord. Furthermore, if we are doing our job and winning the lost, more and more people with such a background will fill our ranks. It is unavoidable in the society in which we live, and missionaries constantly face this problem. Our redemptive mission makes the problem inevitable. Those who are saved are saved to serve, and we have a responsibility to know assuredly how and where they can serve with God's blessing. Therefore everyone is involved, either directly or indirectly, and we are all forced to do some hard and forthright thinking on the subject. The problem belongs to us all, whether we like it or not.

The Church's Redemptive Attitude

Another caution should be observed in approaching the problem. That is to studiously avoid a spirit of self-righteousness and judgment. Only he who is without sin should cast stones or judgmental glances. Jesus alone had this qualification, and yet His attitude toward sinners of every stripe was that of compassion and discipline. He first showed compassionate love and then restoring discipline. Our attitude must be a reflection of His if our service is to be effective.

17

I wonder if we have thoroughly recognized the depth of His compassion and the attitude of the Father toward those who have failed in this regard. If we question that divine concern, it may be that we have forgotten the sad facts He has revealed about His own family relations. He knows well the plight of those who have suffered domestic problems of unfaithfulness, for He Himself suffered the same. For those who have rebellious and delinquent children, for instance, He admits to having had delinquents Himself in Isaiah 1:2. Lamenting through Isaiah, He said, "I have nourished and brought up children, and they have rebelled against me." In spite of His best efforts in love and discipline, they revolted from Him and disowned Him as their Father.

For those who have lost a wife or husband because of unfaithfulness, the Lord understands like you wouldn't believe. He too had that problem, as He admits in the Books of Hosea, Jeremiah, and Ezekiel. To the prophet Hosea, who had an unfaithful wife, the Lord didn't just send condolences. Rather, He solemnly declared that He Himself was reluctantly filing divorce charges against Israel for her idolatry. This court action He states in Hosea 2 and proceeds to elaborate throughout the book. His wail in Hosea 11:8 summarizes His feeling toward the nation and dramatically reflects the sobs of many bereft partners as He exclaims, "How shall I give thee up, Ephraim?" God Himself had to get a divorce because of His beloved's unfaithfulness.

We often forget how intimate His compassion is toward those with marital problems. His concern is a very knowing sympathy, born of experience, not a condescending, judgmental censure. He has personally suffered the same tragedy. No wonder He is called the "God of all comfort" (2 Cor. 1:3) and the "Wonderful Counselor" (Isa. 9:6). He understands the agony of delinquency and divorce in a most realistic way and certainly not as one who is aloof and uninvolved. This reminds us that Isaiah's words, "In all their affliction he was afflicted" (63:9), were not mere words of sentimental rhetoric, but were of the Lord's experience. Through all these experiences, however, God showed the greatness of His longsuffering in solemnly vowing to woo and win back unfaithful Israel to whom He was betrothed. In so doing, He not only outlined Israel's future, but also dramatized the fact that He fully understands every family distress and upheaval. With a classic case of His own in which all hope seemed to have vanished, the Lord showed that no situation is so far gone as to be beyond hope.

The point to be noted is two-pronged. It first emphasizes that no distressed couple or bereft individual needs to approach God as though He were above such human problems and without sympathetic understanding. God is not just a censorious Judge; He is also a compassionate Friend. It also reminds us that such an attitude of understanding and redemptive mercy should likewise characterize the church, unless we have forgotten our redemptive mission. For us to fail to reflect God's attitude of mercy and restoration here is to invite His just judgment upon us, as Jesus declared (Matt. 7:2). God is in the business of helping people where they hurt, and we need to be about our Father's business.

The Various Approaches Taken

The historic positions. On the issue of divorce and remarriage, the church has historically taken many positions. The question has been debated from the time of Christ, and even from the time of Moses. Prior to the Reformation, the prevailing view of the Western church was that marriage was a sacrament performed by God, and therefore no grounds for divorce were recognized except

19

on the basis of nullity. The concept of nullity, rarely and reluctantly used by the Catholic Church, simply pronounced a marriage invalid on the basis that the necessary ingredients of a proper union were not really present to begin with. It was not a truly Christian marriage, in effect. That sacramental view is still theoretically held by them as stated in Canon 1118: "Marriage which is valid and consummated cannot be dissolved by any human power, nor by any cause save death." Thus to divorce and remarry before the death of one partner is to "live in adultery," according to the traditional Roman position.

The Reformers (Luther, Calvin, Knox, Wesley, etc.), on the other hand, did recognize certain legitimate grounds for divorce and remarriage, such as adultery, desertion, and cruelty. These grounds were legitimate, however, only as so judged by the church or corporate body. Since the marriage union is related to God and society, as well as the vowing couple, it was held that the corporate body of the church must also give its approval of a divorce, as well as to an ensuing remarriage. The church represented God and society in joining the couple. This differed from the Catholic position in that it saw marriage as a joining of a couple by society, as well as by God. And since human considerations were involved in approving the union, human involvements should also be considered in a divorce. To put it differently, the Reformers saw that man was not necessarily made for marriage, but that marriage was made for man.

This view of the Reformers has generally been held by most Protestant denominations as being the more biblical. Their sanction of remarriage, however, has usually been restricted to the "innocent party." Concerning the status of the so-called "guilty party," a rather vague and uncertain attitude has been taken. The guilty have been consigned tacitly to some kind of oblivion — no one is quite sure

20

where. Perhaps a form of excommunication best describes their status.

The current rethinking. In the last thirty years most Protestant church bodies have begun to rethink and revise their views on this issue because of the increased influx of divorcees into the church. A variety of forces have combined to precipitate the need to adopt a more restorative or "redemptive" policy toward them. Their place of service in the church also is being reviewed with a more "realistic" or liberal viewpoint, inasmuch as the concept of a first- and second-class membership is quite repugnant to the gospel and grace. It is thought inconsistent to make this marital issue the decisive watermark between public service for Christ and nonservice, since other spiritual characteristics appear to be more greatly emphasized throughout the New Testament.

Thus the church is in the throes of a revolution in its thinking on divorce and remarriage which the social environment has forced upon it. This is fortunate in one way and unfortunate in another. It is always healthy to recheck the biblical grounds of any religious position on which we stand. On the other hand, although theology is partially designed to meet man's social circumstances, it should not be determined by it. Theology ought to be on the leading edge of our social thinking, not dragged into the arena by it. This evidently has not been the case on this crying social issue of our time. Therefore, it is essential that some catching up be done by the church if it is to remain theologically relevant and able to maintain a sound, biblical stance in confronting the problem. The dilemma calls for a forthright word from heaven through a fresh look at the Scriptures.

Recognizing this need for a biblical perspective, various writers have taken another look at the pertinent passages which speak of divorce and remarriage. The crux of

21

the problem is that different conclusions can be drawn from different Bible passages. In the classic texts on the subject, Moses, Christ, and Paul seem to speak differently on the issue. Each seems to give a different allowance for divorce and remarriage. Moses' Old Testament allowance on the ground of "some uncleanness" is unclear, and its meaning was debated even in the time of Christ. In the Gospels Christ appears to grant the legitimacy of divorce and remarriage by the "exception clause" in Matthew, but does not mention it in Mark or Luke. Paul, on the other hand, does not speak of Christ's allowance for divorce, but appears to recognize another legitimate ground, that of desertion. We then are left with the problem of what the Bible does recognize as legitimate grounds for divorce and possible remarriage. Can these passages be harmonized for application today, or were they relevant only in their historical settings?

To reconcile these passages, various approaches have been taken. Most writers have recognized the dispensational nature of the Mosaic legislation and have handily relegated its significance to the pre-Christian era. The words of Christ in the Gospels, however, is where the real rub comes, inasmuch as His words are given in different ways by the synoptic Gospels. To solve this, some interpreters have held Matthew's account as authentic, but not Mark's. Others have maintained Mark's to be the original, and Matthew's troublesome "exception clause" to be an addition by the early church. This is really the "scissors" approach, and the decision as to which passage is to be eliminated appears to be determined by the subjective bias of the interpreter. Such an approach shows its own bankruptcy in attributing contradictions to the texts which it finds disagreeable. Why bother with the text at all if you are going to write off part of it or rewrite it yourself?

Another approach that has gained prominence is to

22

exploit the dispensational character of Jesus' words and thus reduce their binding significance for today. This approach holds a high view of all the gospel texts, but sees Jesus' words on the question of divorce as primarily expressing God's "ideal" for men in terms of the coming kingdom. The strictness of Jesus' law is seen as absolute, but it is really an ideal to be finally realized in the kingdom. Since men today live in human weakness, even the best fall short of the high ideals set forth by Christ. Therefore, according to this view, these ideals should be the believer's pattern to strive for, but not to literally attain in this age of grace. God's redemptive initiative is available to make up for human weakness where conditions so demand. In other words, His absolute law is conditioned and superceded by His grace.

This approach is admittedly a brave attempt to preserve the integrity of Jesus' words on the question of divorce and to harmonize them with His redemptive spirit toward sinners in real life. It is also laudatory in its effort to make Jesus' counsel relevant and related to where the rubber meets the road today. But, although it is well-intentioned, it is extremely questionable in interpretive method. It really is a prostitution of the dispensational method of interpretation. It presents Jesus as saying one thing for the ideal world, while meaning another for the real world about Him. It attributes to Him a "tongue-in-cheek" command which no one can comply with. Applied to the rest of Scripture, it would make God's Word a complete enigma for real life. Try it on John 3:16, which was spoken even before this word from the Sermon on the Mount. Surely a more obvious and simple interpretation can be found that is both scriptural and reasonable.

Others have sought to apply this approach of the "sweet reasonablesss" of Christianity in other ways. They have circumvented the strictness of Jesus' words by viewing them as culturally applying to His own age, but not necessarily binding for today. Since He reputedly spoke in line with the customs of His day, we are to do likewise in line with the culture of our time. We are to take seriously His attitude, rather than His literal words. With this we are to speak "redemptively" and "realistically" to the problems of our day. To bolster this view, they interpret Paul in 1 Corinthians 7, as making further allowances for divorce in line with the needs and distresses of his time. This, as we shall presently see, is a desperate attempt to construct and confirm an attractive alternative for our delinquent age by taking Paul's words out of their context. While the historic setting must always be considered in understanding a passage, that setting does not limit or circumscribe its application, unless specifically declared so in the context. Though our "sweet reasonableness" is certainly essential, it must be the "sweet reasonableness" declared by God.

The popular approach of counselors today then is to be sympathetic and understanding and to speak redemptively and realistically to all marriage problems. The general requisites for remarriage are simply an evaluation of past failures and good, sincere intentions for the rematch. The logic and compassion of this approach is admittedly sound and realistic for our unglued generation, but something is missing for the concerned believer. That something is the biblical authority for it. Without this authority a general uneasiness sooner or later arises to dampen or question the whole relation. The result is that either their consciences have to be squelched, or the biblical authority on the question is discarded as irrelevant for today. And violating either of these inevitably blurs God's line of communication with them and thus also His further will for their lives. Either way, the bargain turns out to be a bad one.

The Biblical Answer

We believe that these modern approaches have made a contribution to solving the problem, but they have not provided the answer. They have admittedly forced us to think redemptively and realistically concerning the home and have flushed us out of our traditional, pat positions. They have served to point us to the gracious character of God and the extension of His redemption to the home. But they have not provided an adequate basis of authority. They have left us "high and dry," without a biblical foundation.

The thrust of the study in these chapters is to show that the Bible does have the answer to all these marital problems, if the various passages on the subject are simply taken in their plain and obvious meanings. No interpretive slight of hand is needed to harmonize them. We believe that a complete harmony of principles can be seen as the succeeding passages are understood in their progressive development throughout the Bible. Each passage simply builds on principles given earlier, and none is to be taken in isolation. The divine Author has not left us with contradictory principles on this burning social issue, but has rather provided a marvelous symphony of marital principles for all time.

Furthermore, these principles turn out to be fully redemptive and realistic in their outworking for today. The Bible counsel is not a burned-out approach, calloused and unsympathetic toward this plight and blight on the modern home. It is a divine, dynamic prescription from the God of all grace. Compassionate concern is its dominant feature. On the other hand, its sympathy and redemption are not of the superficial, easy-way-out variety. The principles are redemptive in a truly redemptive way, not just as cop-out rationalizations. They provide for the true recla-

25

mation of broken homes, in whatever state of disrepair they might be found. And in the process, these principles steer us between two traditional perils always stalking the marriage counselor or the troubled couple. Those perils are the tendency to moral permissiveness on the one hand, and to legalistic callousness on the other. On the practical level, the problem in a nutshell is how we can recognize the propriety of divorce and remarriage of any kind, without giving the "green light" to low morals and permissiveness. The Bible's approach slights neither the doctrinal nor the practical concerns, but brings to bear God's balanced principles of love and discipline.

In the following chapters then, we propose to bring together these biblical principles in their logical order as presented throughout the Bible. To understand the causes and cures of marriage breakup, it is first essential to understand marriage itself as the Bible describes it. Therefore, we shall start with an elucidation of the significance of marriage and its various purposes. With this in mind, we will be able to better understand what the Bible says about marriage breakup and its solution. Concerning this problem of divorce then, a chapter will be given, discussing its propriety and impropriety, according to the Bible. The following chapter will examine the question of remarriage which inevitably follows that of divorce. In reviewing this, we shall bring together the many factors that are involved from the personal, family, and social standpoints. Finally, we will take another hard look at what the Bible says about Christian service and its restrictions for those who have experienced the tragedy of divorce. Through it all we shall attempt to keep before us both the divine perspective of God's purposes and the human dilemma of personal hang-ups and family needs. The Bible is designed to meet man's most intimate needs, and the area of marriage counsel is one of its most neglected specialties.

2
The Purpose of Marriage As Designed by God

Romance is an all-time favorite subject. In both ancient and modern times, stories of love have attracted both the young and the old. The fact is that they really originated in the Bible, the world's oldest literature. Not only is the Bible's central plot the story of God's love, but its continuing drama is peppered with portrayals of human and romantic love. A marriage ceremony begins and ends its pages, and God Himself is in attendance at each. The longest chapter of Genesis (24) describes the acquiring of a bride for Isaac, which was one of the greatest events in the life of Abraham his father. Whole books, such as Ruth, Esther, and Song of Solomon, are, in fact, given over to intriguing episodes of romance, love scenes, and marriage. Our age may pride itself on being romantic, but it by no means has a corner on love stories, as if it invented the novelty. At best, we are only rediscovering it. Solomon, for instance, is not only unchallenged as the all-time lover, but is also unsurpassed as a composer of love songs. We should never forget that love is the Bible's most unique feature, and that true romance is not a devilish device, but a divine delight given to men by God. Love does indeed "make the world go round," and it was God who started it turning.

The First Romance

The plot of the first recorded love story and marriage is found in the Bible's first two chapters. In them a garden wedding is described as being arranged by God Himself who spent eternity planning for it. The home is seen as the end product of His creative genius. He personally united the first couple and gave the first pastoral blessing. The story goes like this: After creating Adam, God assigned him the task of naming the animals of Eden's zoo (Gen. 2:19,20). The intention of God in this assignment was evidently more than just his getting acquainted with Leo the lion, Fido the dog, and Felix the cat. He had a more subtle purpose as He continued the creative process. Adam easily found names suitable for the natures of these animals, but he also found something else. He found personal loneliness and unfulfillment. Seeing his long face after this first assignment, God said: "It is not good for the man to be alone" (Gen. 2:18, NASB). Although He had pronounced everything else He had made to be "good," when He made a bachelor, God admitted it was "not good." Something was definitely missing.

This pronouncement, of course, was simply introductory to His fashioning the woman who was to be Adam's complement and companion. Noting that all the animals had complementary mates, Adam found himself especially alone and unfulfilled. God then proceeded to administer anesthesia, borrowed one of Adam's ribs, and formed the woman. The rib He returned in the charming personality of the woman. Although the Lord certainly could have used more dust as His raw materials for Eve's creation, He chose rather to create her from Adam's body. Perhaps this was to intensify the couple's bond of unity and, in fact, that of the whole race. The ancient divines have often noted that God did not fashion her from Adam's foot-bone, nor from a head-bone (as symbolizing either her dominating man or being dominated by him). Rather, He chose a bone close to the man's heart to symbolize affection. The primary intention seems to be that of her closeness to his heart, both to be protected under his arm and for her to be a protectoress of his inmost life and heart. Their unity and equality are certainly suggested in this creative process. A special divine delicacy might also be drawn from the fact of His not making her from the ground, but from the delicate structure of the man's ribs. At least we can entertain the ennobling idea.

The climax of the story, however, was the union or marriage of Adam and Eve. God brought them together and united them. After uniting them, He commanded them to be "one flesh" and not to be separated (Gen. 2:22-24). Thus the first institution God ordained was that of the home, which reminds us that Jesus also began His earthly ministry by attending a wedding at Cana, bringing blessing to a home (John 2). His concern for the home is always primary, as emphasized throughout the Bible.

God's Purpose in Instituting Marriage

Although many purposes were envisioned by God in the establishing of the marriage relation, several should be highlighted as basic. Recognizing these most foundational purposes will help to give us a proper perspective as we think of the problems of divorce and remarriage, besides that of a properly functioning home.

Propagating the race. The most obvious purpose was that of having children to propagate the race. God's first command to the couple in Eden was, "Be fruitful and multiply, and fill the earth" (Gen. 1:28, NASB). This related them to physical nature in its inherent ability to reproduce. It also served to keep the race fresh.

This mating command introduces us to God's general

29

principle of involving men and women as workers together with Him. He didn't just fill the earth with multitudes of people as He did the heavens with angels. In the creative process of men He assigned men, in turn, to be procreators with Him in furthering His creative work. Not that it was to be done in a haphazard way, but only according to God's direction. This life-begetting function He assigned to the married couple alone, and He jealously guards this restriction with warnings of dire consequences to offenders. Both the giving and taking of life are His sacred prerogatives, and the delegating of these responsibilities are strictly assigned by Him. Thus, within the marriage relationship God carries out His further creative process in a fellowship with men. It is altogether fitting and consistent with God's creative work that this life-begetting experience should be one of joy. Didn't all the angels of God shout and sing at His first creation (Job 38:4-7)? The forming of a new personality in God's image is an artistic creation of the highest order. But it is a divine privilege delegated by God to a married couple and should be solemnly recognized as such. In this sense they are workers together with God as He furthers His creation.

Promoting personality growth and grace. The marriage relation, however, is not just a medium of God to propagate the race. He could have done that through other means, as with the angels. The more immediate purpose is concerned with the couple themselves. That purpose is to develop and mature two different personalities in a relationship of mutual fellowship and responsibilities. This is not to suggest the fiction of their marrying and living "happily ever after" without a fuss. That happens only in storybook fantasies. The real life marriage of the Bible doesn't necessarily promise a dream life of perpetual bliss. God never promised a rose garden here on earth. Marriage is rather the joining together of two individuals of opposite sexes who vow to live, love, and work together through rain and shine, sickness and health, or come what may throughout life. They are partners in shaping and maturing each other for eternity.

To this marriage union each comes with a unique personality. Each has a complex of problems or hang-ups and an endowment of gifts or talents in varying degrees of development. No two people have the same tastes or habits. After the honeymoon, it is sometimes traumatically discovered that the gears don't all mesh without squeaking, one zigs when the other zags, and the anticipated harmony and heaven don't seem to materialize. It is easy for two well-intentioned lovers to experience creeping disenchantment after the cosmetics begin to rub off and the eyeball meets the burnt toast. The feeling may gradually develop that "we weren't really meant for each other — we're incompatible."

Popular though this excuse may be today, it really is a genuine cop-out. Marriage partners are not custom made. This disenchantment of a couple with each other can be traced to a wrong conception of the purpose of marriage. They somehow misread the "catalog description" of the marriage game both as to its price and its product. There is a price to pay in terms of personal desires and peculiarities. Regardless how identical their background or makeup, no couple will automatically blend immediately in perfect symphonic harmony. Especially not today with all the pressures and irritations that confront a couple as they comb out the rice to face and tough out life together. If they think they have no problems or personality difficulties to work out together, they are in trouble. They have missed one of the real purposes of marriage. The purpose of life, including marriage, is not just to frolic in the sun and experience monotonous bliss in a life de-

31

void of hardships, adjustments, and problems. That fiction is purely secular and is, in fact, godless and spineless. Christ never promised that for the Christian life, and the marriage experience is no exception. The more primary purpose of marriage is that of growth and personality development. And growth comes through struggle.

It should be recognized that every individual created by God is a diamond in the rough. Diamonds, however, need grinding and polishing to develop their beauty. For this purpose God instituted the marriage relation as one of the central workshops in which that grinding and polishing process takes place. The dust and sparks may have to fly a bit in the workshop, but the two need each other in the refining process just as the diamond needs the grindstone. And the submitting of each partner to this polishing operation is the key to both marriage harmony and their individual development in the plan of God. This is what Paul had in mind in Ephesians 5:21 as he counseled both husbands and wives: "Be subject to one another in the fear of Christ" (NASB). Though each has specific gifts and responsibilities, neither is to be adamant and unsubmissive in responding to the other. The ability to submit and "flex with the punches" (figuratively, we hope) is an essential Christian virtue, and the marriage relation is one of God's ideal arenas in which to practice and perfect the art.

This personality refinement or "diamond honing" calls into play the great Christian graces which God makes available to believers. Love, of course, is the most fundamental, and this should beget a whole array of complementing virtues. From it should spring personal sacrifice, graciousness, consideration, patience, tolerance, cheerfulness, mutual trust, and encouraging suggestions. It should also inspire each to a personal self-inventory. A believer's habits, attitudes, and personal progress in Christian maturity should be subject to periodic appraisal. This love relation should instill a willingness to adjust or respond to the other's need or suggestions. Such responding results in both personal and mutual benefits, better fitting each both for this life and the life to come. This doesn't mean a whimsical acquiescing to every disagreement in a milquetoast fashion or as a piece of spineless putty. It is rather learning to face one's own peculiarities and attitudes in an objective and realistic way. It is listening for God's counsel as He speaks through the one nearest and dearest to you.

This, by the way, was Malachi's point as he denounced the plural marriages of the Israelites (2:14-16). Why, he asks, did God create only one wife for Adam? Was the Spirit exhausted? Did He run out of ribs? Of course not. He established monogamous marriages to promote godliness in the home and the nation. Therefore, he said, God hates divorce, for it is basically a repudiation of God's counsel through the partner in favor of a seemingly less demanding adjustment. God ordained that two people should "rub together," so to speak, in intimate relations to provoke each other unto love and good works.

Viewed in this way, the marriage relation then becomes a most significant divine arrangement in which a couple seeks to shape their individual personalities for eternity. Problems and grievances they didn't know they had are brought to the surface and confronted. In wholesome and intimate communication, they tactfully help each other to "see themselves as others see them." They serve as revealing mirrors for each other. Since we can take only so much of either praise or prodding at a time, the gift of knowing when to turn the mirror on or off is certainly an essential part of the gift of love. Properly given and properly received, however, their mutual counsel tends to remove character blemishes and to bring out the individual potential and glory of each other.

The recognition of this divine purpose in marriage of maturing each other then becomes also a boon to their potential as an effective team. They can see each other as a gift from God for their mutual service together. Rather than being jealous of each other, they can be proud of each other. In this way they enjoy the excellencies of each other and seek to supplement the other's deficiencies in the most effective and tactful way. As the apostle Peter says, the married couple can view themselves as "fellow-heirs" of the grace of life, each complementing the other for the glory of God (1 Peter 3:7). Though having different roles, they serve as a team pulling together and can enjoy even the rigors of the pull.

It is thus evident that the purpose of growing and maturing together through life is one of the great designs of marriage in the divine plan. The relationship is not just for procreation or recreation, but for recreation. It is furthering God's creative process of conforming each other more and more into the image of God (2 Peter 1:4-11). In a sense, it is dying to self, but rising together with your partner in a new "one-flesh" marital union.

Fulfilling man's God-given passions. A third purpose of marriage needs to be noted as indicated by both Christ and Paul. That is the purpose of fulfilling the legitimate sexual passions which God has built into man. This purpose is related to the previously noted one of propagating the race, but is certainly not limited to that. The passions do not automatically subside when child-bearing for a couple is ended. Paul recognized this fact in 1 Corinthians 7:5 by exhorting: "Stop depriving one another, except by agreement for a time that you may devote yourselves to prayer, and come together again lest Satan tempt you because of your lack of self-control" (NASB). The apostle saw this as a legitimate and necessary function of the marriage relation and gave this admonition to married

34

couples, not as a suggestion, but as a command (in the imperative).

It should be noted further that Paul saw the possession of such sexual drives as one of the divine reasons for which God has instituted the marriage relationship. To prevent an improper expression of these passions, the apostle commanded, "let each man have his own wife, and let each woman have her own husband" (1 Cor. 7:2, NASB). Although this chapter in 1 Corinthians often is thought of as Paul's great treatise on the greater benefits of being single, it is here also that he solemnly commands marriage for many and shows why it is physically necessary. That reason is that the couple might give proper expression to their God-given sexual needs (1 Cor. 7:2,9).

This possession or nonpossession of sexual passions Paul declares to be the individual's "gift" from God (1 Cor. 7:7). He recognizes that all people do not have the same personal endowments in this regard and that it is to be subjectively determined by each person individually. In the discussion he extols the virtues of the single state, inasmuch as he himself was single and found that state to be quite conducive to service for God. This defense of singlehood, however, should be seen in light of the historic setting in which Paul wrote. The Jews traditionally saw marriage as both a responsibility and a necessity in order to secure God's blessing in life. To not have children often was considered a curse, and to have children one obviously had to be married. It should also be noted that, in the previous chapter, Paul had denounced sexual immorality and its relation to heathen worship in Corinth. Therefore, in chapter 7 the apostle makes a strong defense for the state of being single and living a life of non-sexual activity. In so doing he acknowledges the propriety of marriage, but seeks to show that the single state is also a most legitimate and desirable state (v. 7).

The emphasis of Paul throughout this discussion in 1 Corinthians 7, however, should not be missed among the many details of marital instructions. That basic emphasis is twofold: 1) whether single or married, the goal of pleasing the Lord should always be uppermost; 2) pleasing the Lord should be pursued by seeking the happiness and spiritual effectiveness of each believer. His emphasis on pleasing the Lord is especially noted in verses 17, 32, 34, and 35. This was obviously his supreme concern. The secondary emphasis, however, also should not be overlooked, for it contributes to the first. This emphasis on the happiness of the believer, married or single, is noted in many places (e.g., vv. 7,26,28,32,36, and 40). He considers their different degrees of self-control, their freedom from trouble, their own profit, and their personal happiness. Thus the decision of whether a person should marry or not Paul leaves with the individual's personal judgment. Each must determine his own "gift" as to whether he or she has sexual needs that cry out for expression. The apostle put it this way: "But if they do not have self-control, let them marry; for it is better to marry than to burn" with passions (1 Cor. 7:9, NASB). He saw no necessary piety in either the lack of passions or the gift of passions. Neither the married state or the single state, as such, are either godly or ungodly. Rather than establishing some divine order of preference, Paul simply stressed the happiness of the individual or couple in serving the Lord.

This clarification by Paul helps us also to understand Christ's point in Matthew 19 on the question of whether or not one should marry. In answer to the disciples' query as to whether the single state might be the better course (to avoid the problems of marital unfaithfulness), Jesus declared that the decision is strictly an individual one. It depends on one's gift from God (Matt. 19:1-12). While celibacy is not generally advisable, there are three excep-

tions which may make it the better course in the will of
God. One is the exception of being born a "eunuch," making marriage inadvisable. The second is the case where
surgery might have been performed, changing the person's sexual needs and abilities. Third, one may have
received the gift of self-control to better promote the kingdom of God (Matt. 19:12). Such was apparently the case of
the apostles Paul and Barnabas, who gave up their right to
matrimony in order to better conduct their missionary
work (1 Cor. 9:5).

In summary, Jesus stressed the fact that neither state is
necessarily preferable, but that each person must decide
the question for himself by evaluating the gifts that God
has given him. To counter any suggestions the disciples
might have developed from the previous discussion that
marriage is carnal, the Lord ended His instruction here by
blessing little children who were obviously the fruit of
marriage. What a beautiful object lesson! Though both the
married and single states have their problems, both also
have their compensations as each person determines the
will of God for his life. Thus the Bible sees marriage and
the fulfilling of one's sexual passions within that union as
a gift from God, not as a pandering to the carnal seductions
of sin or the sin nature. That union is a holy one, for it was
established by God.

Typifying Christ's marriage to the church. A final
purpose of marriage is suggested in Paul's counsel to the
church in Ephesians 5. As he there gives instruction to
husbands and wives, he also declares that the marriage
relationship is really a type or picture of the coming union
of Christ with His church. In at least six ways Paul relates
the marriage of husband and wife to that of Christ's relation to His church family (Eph. 5:22-32). In fact, he speaks
of the first marriage in Eden as being a prefiguring of this
divine-human relationship. The mystery of two lovers be-

coming "one flesh" in marriage he describes as being especially fulfilled in Christ's coming marriage to the church.

This cosmic and divine relationship gives marriage a whole new perspective. It puts it on the highest plane imaginable. It declares that God is specifically using the institution of marriage to portray that eternal union of Christ the Son of God with His people, the church. No event in all the divine calendar is as important as this coming event in which the Father will consummate the union of His Son with His "glorious bride" (Eph. 5:27). Although the human relations are temporal and preparatory, the divine-human relation will be permanent and completely fulfilling. And the people that make up that bride are those whom God is seeking today as He builds His church. They will forever be His closest companions as He reigns over the universe and institutes the high adventures of His eternal enterprises and delights.

No wonder then that the high ideals of faithfulness, purity, and love are strictly enjoined on the marriage relationship! They portray Christ's relation with His eternal bride, a relationship of the highest order. That is why we are to love each other in spite of differences, for we dimly portray Christ's love for the church. Paul strongly implies that this is one of the principal purposes of marriage in the divine program. Even the purpose of propagating the race is really subsidiary to this divine portrayal of Christ's eternal relationship with His people.

Thus the ostensible name of the game is "marriage," but its purpose is often misunderstood. If you don't believe it, try asking a couple why they got married, and prepare yourself for a shock. (Try it on yourself first.) The real purpose of marriage is to reflect, in a typical way, the love relation between God and His people and to implant and perfect that love in human personalities. Marriage is God's workshop or garden in which He is growing and maturing personalities for eternity. This purpose should be recognized by every Christian couple so that the "ups and downs" of their marriage experience can be taken in proper stride. The anticipated "rose garden" can materialize only as God is recognized as the Gardener and the pruning and praising processes are properly appreciated. The fragrance and beauty of the relationship are brought out by their mutual discipline and delights in the plan of God.

3
God's Word on the Breaking of Wedlock

Although the marriage relation enjoys God's special ordination and promises the height of human bliss, it sometimes falls flat and doesn't deliver. Ordained to be a "little taste of heaven on earth," it at times becomes a little taste of something else. An ungluing process can easily set in that separates first the affections and finally the entire marriage. No problem, in fact, is more prevalent or destructive in our society than this one of marriage breakup. Though it has had periods of great prevalency in ancient times and cultures, it is especially snowballing in our permissive age at all levels of society. And believers are by no means immune to the disease. Probably no problem is more familiar to the pastor or counselor and none more difficult to solve than when a breakup occurs.

Our purpose here, however, is not to discuss the various causes or remedies propounded. The social experts have written lengthily and wisely on the subject, filling our bookshelves with counsel. We propose rather to simply gather together the basic principles of the Bible on the issue so that the believer might have a clear understanding of his responsibilities concerning marriage and divorce. A variety of questions confronts us. Is the Bible concerned with the issue of marriage breakup on the practical level?

Or does it merely whitewash the question with statements of idealism? Does it realistically recognize divorce? How permanent is marriage in the eyes of God? If divorce is allowed, what are its proper grounds? When it does occur, what is the believer's first responsibility? What are the church's responsibilities? Is the option of remarriage legitimate to consider, and when is one "living in sin"? What is the redemptive hope for marriage failures and how extensive is it? Are the teachings of the Old and New Testaments contradictory or consistent on the subject? What are the abiding principles?

Believing that the Bible speaks decisively to the moral problems of our age, we should expect this crucial area to be clearly treated with a minimum of uncertain sounds. Let's put together the various passages that deal with the subject and notice the principles taught.

In pursuing these biblical principles, it is helpful to look at them in what appears to be their most logical order. The areas to be discussed then will be: 1) the achieving of peace and reconciliation in marriage; 2) the recourse when unfaithfulness occurs; 3) the biblical options open to divorced people; 4) the propriety of remarriage; and 5) the place of Christian service for those who have had marriage failures. The first two are related and will be considered together in this chapter.

The Principle of Communication and Reconciliation

When a marriage begins to sour and the early stages of disenchantment set in, it is especially important that a couple recognize their God-given responsibilities and resources. These may be thought of as *self-evaluation* and *spouse-evaluation* with the accompanying resources for making responses.

Self-evaluation. As previously noted, no marriage is without its problems in terms of personality clashes and adjustments. This follows from both the sinful rascality of all men and the individual peculiarities of even the best of Christian men and women. Tailor-made mates who fulfill all one's matrimonial dreams are just not on the market. Furthermore, "Play-Doh" personalities or mates without individual desires and convictions do not have the resilient qualities of which good marriages are made. Therefore, adjustments in give-and-take compromises are to be expected in a well-ordered relationship. To recognize the need for such adjustments is half the battle; and to refuse to recognize it is the beginning of another battle, a disastrous one.

The place for each marriage partner to begin these adjustments is with himself, not with his spouse. The Bible instructs the husband to attend to his own responsibility of loving his wife, not to be the dean of education for her instruction. He is not told to require submission of his wife, nor is the wife told to demand his love (Eph. 5:21ff.). The urge to counsel and instruct is native to all of us and we are prone to practice the felony on those closest to us. But, as charity begins at home, so charitable understanding toward one's God-given mate is the place to start. Each is to evaluate his own responsibilities and fulfill them, recognizing that this is designed to evoke a similar evaluation and response on the part of his partner.

The peril of reversing this process and each acting as a kind of provost marshall over the other is often warned against in the Bible. Christ and Paul both warned against the general sin of a censorious spirit, suggesting this as tantamount to playing God to your neighbor (Matt. 7:1; Rom. 14:4,13). We all have an uncanny ability to see our own faults in other people, and the "speck" in their eye often turns out to be a "log" in our own (Matt. 7:3).

More specifically, the Book of Proverbs refers to contention in the home, and does it with some pretty salty

43

illustrations. In speaking of a "backbiting tongue," the writer declares, "It is better to live in a corner of the roof than in a house shared with a contentious woman" (Prov. 25:23,24, NASB). In Proverbs 27:15 he portrays this contention as a "constant dripping on a day of steady rain" (NASB). The picture is one of incessant nagging which drives the partner either out of the house (if not out of his mind) or to the remotest den of refuge in the attic or cellar. If this reference appears to be chauvinistic, suggesting only a womanly vice, the real point has been missed, for his analogy is only for emphasis. His portrait of the virtuous woman in the last chapter more than compensates for his using the figure of the foolish woman throughout the book in emphasizing his point. The lesson of what nagging and constant critical appraisal of one's partner will do is obviously two-pronged. Men are not less adept at the game than women.

The point to be noted is that anyone who practices fault-finding toward his partner usually has developed a blind spot to his own defects. This was the sin of the finger-pointing Pharisees and Jesus called them short in John 8:7 by saying, "He who is without sin among you, let him be the first to throw a stone at her" (NASB). It is remarkable how a little self-inventory tends to improve our patience with others and to remind us that we too are human. While helping each one to initiate necessary self-improvements, it also cultivates a gracious atmosphere for both to be objective and realistic. Self-evaluation then is the first solid plank in the building of a platform of good marital relations.

Spouse-evaluation. Evaluation of one's self, however, is not the whole story, and one would be remiss to stop there. Introspection by itself breeds neuroses. We are also, in a sense, our "brother's keeper," and our marital partner's as well. While Jesus instructed us not to judge our neighbor with a "log" in our own eye, He did not deny us the responsibility of helping him with his problems. After attending to self-judgment, Jesus said, you can then "see clearly enough to take the speck out of your brother's eye" (Matt. 7:5, NASB). In other words, be sure the failure you see in your neighbor is real, not just imagined or a projection of your own. The same goes for marital relations.

In evaluating one's spouse, his or her strengths and weaknesses are to be fully appreciated and recognized. Everyone has his idiosyncrasies which are native to his personality, and everyone has his special gifts. The apostle Peter admonished husbands to dwell with their wives "according to knowledge, giving honour unto the wife, as unto the weaker vessel" (1 Peter 3:7, KJV). Their natural abilities and limitations are to be taken into account, which includes their varying tastes and backgrounds. But he also alluded to the responsibility of considering their differing spiritual backgrounds and progress. Wives, for instance, can win their unsaved husbands, not by harping at them with a string of Bible verses, but by living a gracious and understanding life before them (1 Peter 3: 1-4). And Christian couples also have different levels of spiritual maturity which should be recognized. It is immature and naive on the part of one partner to demand spiritual maturity on the part of the other. It doesn't come that way. Forced growth by reprimand and cajoling is more destructive and stultifying than wholesome. It denigrates the ego by dragging rather than leading, and produces only superficial compliances. Personality growth and spiritual development must come from within. A discerning Christian will keep this in mind and not assume the role of being the architect of his partner's personality remodeling. Rather, Christians will accept their partner for what he or she is and simply be an encouragement to them in their own self-evaluation and improvement.

The divine resources. Thus, the manner in which the "speck" is extricated from the partner's eye is the real rub. This is where living together becomes an art as well as a science. But the Christian couple has a definite edge in practicing the art in that they are provided with some special spiritual resources. One is that of daily exposure to the Word of God as they read and study it together. In those sessions around the Scriptures, Christ is recognized as Lord of the home and His instruction speaks to each one individually. They are reminded together of God's will for their lives and of the resources and power He makes available for building a Christian home together.

The second resource of Christian partners in dealing with problems they see in each other is the example technique of holy behavior. We have noted this in 1 Peter, where Peter refers to it as a dynamic incentive to promote both peace and spiritual progress in the home. He even suggests that Sarah (with all her questionable ideas) made a contribution to Abraham's spiritual development. Abraham's faith wasn't perfected by himself. The point is that the effect of a quiet and consistent life before one's partner is a living translation of God's Word, bound to be read.

The third and most important resource available is that of prayer. This avenue is pointed to many times in the Bible, but is especially cogent as John relates it in 1 John 5:16. He there declares that "If any one sees his brother committing a sin not leading to death, he shall ask and God will give life to those who commit sin not leading to death" (NASB). Aside from the interpretive problem of the "sin unto death," the passage strongly reminds us of our first responsibility when we note a defect in our neighbor — or our spouse. That responsibility is to pray. The usual response is to ridicule, rebuke, carp, or tell him what he should do or where he should go. All this is only ego-destroying and makes for defensive reactions. It shows that we are on the same spiritual level as he is, only with different defects. We rebuke a person for using the same fleshly resources that we use, only less effectively. In our impatience we forget that our real resource is spiritual. God gave us prayer to move men as well as mountains. Without it our other efforts are useless. Furthermore, the results of using the resource of prayer John declares to be certain (1 John 5:16). The Lord will assuredly give correction to an erring neighbor or partner if we make the petition, for it is always His will to correct and mature His people.

Prayer then makes unlimited the possibilities of Christian partners building each other up. It is an enterprise in which we can be workers together with God. As we observe areas of need, immaturity, or sin in our partners, our immediate recourse is to God who knows all the circumstances and who is able to mysteriously work from within. This removes the unwholesome atmosphere of judgmental attitudes and avoids the depressive problem of ego breakdown or defensiveness which is always a barrier to personality growth. It tends to foster an atmosphere of grace and dependence on the Lord which both husband and wife can appreciate as the marital problems are resolved. Even through difficult problems we can have that peace to which God has called marriage partners. "O what peace we often forfeit! . . . what needless pain we bear!"

When Unfaithfulness Occurs

As with many other human experiences, however, we tend to play the marriage game by ear, rather than by the directions of biblical principles. When all else fails, we frantically look for the directions, often too late. Because the biblical principles of peace, growth, and reconciliation are not observed, a breakdown in communication and

47

affections often occurs. In our society especially, this easily leads to unfaithfulness in a resort to other relationships. Infidelity in the marriage bond often results. For whatever cause it happens, it is a mounting problem, and we should know what the Bible says about it. Although both parties inevitably contribute to the defection, the sin of adultery usually begins with one partner being guilty of the actual offense. It is a cop-out for the adulterous party to use the lame excuse that "he (or she) drove me to it," and thus both are guilty. The Bible knows of no such jurisprudence, though other failures may obviously have aggravated the immoral act. The Bible holds the participating pair themselves to be the guilty ones. The question then arises as to what the "innocent party" should do when he or she discovers the unfaithfulness of the partner. What are the legitimate options that the Bible allows?

Divorce may be necessary. The very thought of divorce is abhorrent to all believers. To those personally involved, it often is worse than death itself. (This often is true also for unbelievers.) What realistic approach does the Bible give to this problem? We should first of all recognize that it does not present it as an option, but as a last resort, if not a last rite. Adultery called for death under the Mosaic legislation. While the Old Testament allowed divorce for certain, limited reasons, it was because of the sin of hardness or the inflexibility of the partners to be reconciled. Malachi stoutly declared that the Lord hates divorce (Mal. 2:16). Furthermore, Christ in Matthew 19:4-6 affirmed the divine intention that marriage was to be a lifelong relationship. "What therefore God has joined together," He said, "let no man separate" (NASB).

We then are driven to ask whether divorce is ever a legitimate Christian action or is even recognized by God. When the civil courts grant a couple a divorce, does God grant it, or does He see the couple as still married? To see

48

the full biblical perspective we need to consider both the Old Testament foundations and the New Testament clarifications. The key Old Testament passage on this issue is Deuteronomy 24, and it is also that to which the New Testament refers as the problem is confronted. In that passage Moses gave Israel its regulations concerning the place and limitations of divorce. Far from revising God's original intention for permanent marriage ties, he rather set limitations on a rampant practice of divorce that was developing. This he did by restricting its use to an exceptional moral cause and by requiring a written document to make it legal. In this legislation, Moses actually provided the woman involved with a degree of protection by requiring its review and legal action. It also served to remind the husband that he would lose her forever when he got a divorce in that culture. Even though her next husband should die, the former husband could never remarry her, for God regarded that as an abomination (Deut. 24:4; Jer. 3:1).

From this Old Testament legislation it is to be noted that God did recognize divorce when it took place in Israel's courts, even though the union was designed to be permanent. Moses spoke of the woman becoming "another man's wife" and of her first husband as being her "former husband" (Deut. 24:2,3). And if God recognized divorce as severing a relationship in the Old Testament, there is no indication that He denies that it may happen in the New Testament. Christ, in fact, referred the Pharisees to Moses' law when they questioned Him on the subject (Mark 10:2,3). Although God saw sin to be the cause of marriage dissolution, He did recognize the possibility of it occurring.

The legitimate cause of divorce. If God recognizes that certain sins may indeed bring about divorce, as noted by Moses and Jesus, we should then identify what those sins

49

are. What does the Bible recognize as legitimate grounds for a believer to seek a divorce? We note first that Jesus' statement in Mark 10 does not elaborate on this, for that was not the focus of Mark's point there. In Matthew 19, however, the discussion is given in more detail where the specific question of the proper grounds for divorce is asked. That ground, Jesus explained, was the infidelity or adultery of the other partner. He had previously alluded to this in the Sermon on the Mount (Matt. 5:32), and here further elucidates it in response to a specific question. This, by the way, was not some interim ethic, as some would suggest, for Jesus was now on His way to the cross and had already announced His plan to build His church (Matt. 16:18).

There are many who have called into question the authenticity of this passage in Matthew, since it gives some details not given by Mark or Luke. The ground for questioning it, however, is purely subjective, for it has the strongest manuscript support in the Greek texts. Though many ingenious ways have been used to void it, the passage has been overwhelmingly acknowledged as authentic by the great textual scholars of history. If we recognize that God is the Author of all four gospel accounts and that they supplement each other in their various details, the variation difficulty disappears. Whereas Mark and Luke give summary accounts of Jesus' teaching on the subject, Matthew gives a detailed account, noting also the specific question asked and the more specific answer given by Jesus. This is characteristic of Matthew in recording Jesus' teaching, as evident in the Sermon on the Mount and the Olivet Discourse. His additional details on the divorce issue, then are totally reliable and entirely consistent with the shorter accounts.

The unique addition supplied by Matthew here is the "exception clause," which is given in both Matthew 5:32

and 19:9. It will help to recite both passages to get their full impact. Matthew 5:32 says: ". . . but I say to you that every one who divorces his wife, except for the cause of unchastity, makes her commit adultery; and whoever marries a divorced woman commits adultery" (NASB). Matthew 19:9 says: "And I say to you, whoever divorces his wife, except for immorality, and marries another commits adultery" (NASB).

In the first instance Jesus declares that a man becomes guilty of two counts of adultery when he divorces his wife; he makes both her and the one she later marries commit adultery in the act of their marrying. In the second instance, He asserts that a man commits adultery personally when he divorces his wife and marries another woman. This warning of the sin of committing adultery by divorce is obviously the main thrust of Jesus' two statements on the subject. Mark 10:12 adds the fact that the woman also might initiate the divorce and thus commit adultery. The solemnity of Jesus' words in these warnings is crystal clear and must not be watered down by deceptive rationalizations. They are definitive statements and are as binding and enduring as John 3:16. Divorce is definitely not God's way of resolving marriage problems.

But the exception which Jesus included in both statements is just as binding and must not be overlooked. That exception is where one or both of the partners have been involved in *porneia* (fornication, immorality, unchastity, etc.). What does the term mean? In the Old Testament the equivalent term, *zanah*, almost universally meant adultery. In the New Testament the term is used twenty-six times, referring to all types of illicit sexual intercourse (Arndt and Gingrich's *Greek-English Lexicon of the New Testament*). It is a broader term than "adultery" (*moicheia*), but often includes it. Jesus evidently used the term *porneia* here, rather than *moicheia*, to show the

51

disastrous effect of any illicit sexual relations on the marriage relationship.

Adultery then has the effect of aborting or dissolving a marriage union in the eyes of God. Though the marriage was designed by God to be permanent or life-long, the act of adultery breaks the one-flesh union of husband and wife in defiance of the will of God. As Paul said, "the one who joins himself to a harlot is one body with her" (1 Cor. 6:16, NASB). This being true, the other partner is not guilty of adultery when getting a divorce. Adultery in that case has already been committed, and has severed the union by the breach of faithfulness and a new physical union.

The conclusion that Jesus saw adultery as the one legitimate ground for a couple being divorced thus is almost unavoidable. This view, of course, was similar to the position taken by the school of Shammai in Jesus' time, though it is more specific in naming the sin of *porneia*. (The school of Hillel, it will be recalled, allowed divorce by the man for almost any cause or point of irritation.) With respect to the law of Moses, there is little evidence that Jesus altered the Old Testament legislation concerning God's view of divorce. He explicitly said that He came not to destroy Moses' law or the prophets, but to "fill it out," in regard to its principles (Matt. 5:17,18). The Jews had for centuries debated the exact meaning of the "some indecency" which Moses delineated as ground for divorce in Deuteronomy 24:1. Though it may not have been actual adultery (which required the death penalty, according to Deut. 22:22), it evidently involved some type of illicit sex coupled with deception. (Not all sex crimes were punishable by death as noted in Exod. 22:16,17; Deut. 22:25-29.) Jesus, however, did not need to annul the death penalty for sex crimes, for that was already voided when Israel lost her theocratic status in 605 B.C. and the "times of the Gentiles" began. Their Gentile overlords did not require death for adultery and the Jews were divinely subjected to their civil laws (Rom. 13:1). Jesus' point, then, was simply to reiterate the disastrous effect that a fornicatory relation imposes on one's marriage. It constitutes its death knell, as it also did in Old Testament times.

This clarification by Jesus, however, should not be seen as allowing laxity in granting loopholes for divorce. It was rather intended to emphasize the devastating effect of extramarital sex. In God's eyes such a relation breaks the one-flesh union which He established. The evidence for the Roman Catholic fiction that marriage is indissoluble under any circumstance is built on extremely questionable grounds. It appeals primarily to "Peter's gospel through Mark," and overlooks the more detailed account by Matthew. The Reformers almost unanimously took issue with this view and recognized the testimony of Matthew that adultery does break the marriage relation. Jesus was not highlighting a legitimate loophole for divorce, but was sounding a solemn warning concerning adultery. This sin, He warned, has the effect of destroying a marriage and a home.

The will of God for reconciliation. Since adultery is pronounced so devastating by Jesus, we are driven to inquire more carefully into the legitimacy of divorce. Is it ever proper for a Christian to seek divorce? We should first of all recognize that, although "God hates divorce" (Mal. 2:16), there is something He hates even more. That something is the cause for which He allows divorce, which is, an adulterous relation. This He considers intolerable. The divorced woman of Deuteronomy 24, for instance, was not to go back to her husband after marrying another, under any circumstances. In other words, she was not to be passed back and forth in a dual relationship as in a barnyard situation. That constituted abomination in the sight of God (Deut. 24:4).

53

The lesson to be drawn from both the words of Moses and the warning of Jesus, then, is that there may be times when divorce (or at least separation) is the will of God for an innocent party. If one's marriage partner is playing the harlot or the tomcat with someone else, it is more of a sin to continue to live with that one than to separate. To be submissive to such an arrangement by condoning it is to be a party to it. One should lay down the law to the erring partner and refuse to continue the union. The sinning partner needs to be severely jolted and reminded of the enormity of his or her crime. God doesn't condone such behavior, and He holds us responsible not to tolerate it either. To be timid here is to promote the abomination that God hates worse than divorce.

In taking this action, however, it should be recognized that reconciliation is the primary desire of God. Though divorce or separation may be required to call a halt to an abominable situation of dual sex, the case may not be entirely lost. Admitting from the evidence of Jesus' words that divorce is permissible and may be necessary when a partner is unfaithful, the believer who has tasted of God's forgiving grace may want to extend that grace to the partner who has sinned against him or her as well as against God. He may want to go the second mile in overlooking a fault to fill a need by extending unmerited forgiveness. Such forgiveness, of course, should be only on the basis of proper repentance both to God and to all those involved. It should be a repentance which vows anew a couple's faithfulness to each other in the marriage relationship. Anything less would be a mockery and an invitation to re-write the odious chapter in another extramarital relationship.

The believer, furthermore, should never conceive of reconciliation as an impossibility, unless the other party has remarried or is living in a common-law situation. This is the lesson the Lord impressed on Hosea the prophet who had a wife that became a harlot. Though having every right to divorce and completely renounce her according to the law of Moses, he was counseled by God to extend grace instead of judgment in an unprecedented way. And the evidence, in the analogy of the book, indicates that that grace shown by Hosea paid off in a new and beautiful relationship. Grace always pays high dividends sooner or later. Likewise, the believer today who faces such a situation can effect a similar reconciliation and renewed relation. It can be effected by appropriating the spiritual resources that God has made available, especially those of prayer and patience. If the situation appears impossible, we are reminded that "with God nothing shall be impossible" (Luke 1:37, KJV). To humbly beseech God for such reconciliation is to move the arm of God who works miracles, for we can always be sure that reconciliation of marriage partners is His will.

How about desertion? We must further ask whether adultery is the only biblical ground for divorce. It has been widely held by many Protestant churches that the desertion of one partner also constitutes proper ground for divorce by the other. This was the position of most of the Reformers, and most denominations and pastors recognize it also today. Other grounds such as impotence, cruelty, and religious incompatibility have been invoked by many, but not with nearly the acceptance that desertion has had.

It should be recognized that the crime of desertion can admittedly be even more vicious and debilitating to a home than adultery. The deprivations it incurs are often like that of death itself as far as the family is concerned. Furthermore, the problem of desertions in the United States is currently so monumental that its cases in 1975 are said to have equaled that of legal divorces (Andre Bustanoby, *Christianity Today*, June, 1975). This being true, it is essential to know how the Bible regards it and what the church's attitude should be in dealing with it.

The primary reference in the New Testament is 1 Corinthians 7:10-15, which deals also with religious incompatibility. In that passage Paul gave instruction concerning marriage separations, especially where an unbelieving partner is involved. The probable situation was that in which one member of an unsaved couple became saved and the other remained unsaved. The question then arose as to whether this constituted an unholy union and ought to be terminated by the saved member. That procedure, of course, would play havoc with marriages where only one partner becomes saved. Paul's instruction was definitely in the negative. He rather declared that the salvation of the one actually sanctified the whole family in a sense, by providing the impetus for their later salvation. In such a case the unsaved mate and family became a mission field from which the saved partner should not run away. Thus he disallowed religious incompatibility as legitimate ground for which believers may seek divorce.

On the other hand, the unbelieving partner might desert and leave the believer in a divorced situation for all practical purposes. What then is the deserted believer to do, inasmuch as the apostle had just instructed couples to remain together? How far must the believing partner go to keep the union intact and retain the blessing of God on their lives?

Paul's answer to this was that the believer "is not under bondage in such cases, but God has called us to peace" (1 Cor. 7:15, NASB). Our problem then is to discover what Paul meant by being "not under bondage" (*ou dedoulotai*). This phrase has been much discussed in church history, and there is certainly no general concensus even today. Does this freedom from bondage mean complete

56

freedom from the marriage tie and also the accompanying freedom to remarry? Or does it mean a more restricted freedom for the estranged partner in the event of desertion? Whichever view one takes, it is evident that the apostle recognizes that such a desertion might take place and thus thrust the believer into a state of practical divorce, not the fault of his own. Following Christ, as the Lord declared, may involve the loss of family and even one's wife (Matt. 19:29) or husband. Whether it does, in fact, mean complete freedom from the marriage bond, Paul's primary point appears to be the idea of freedom from guilt or the responsibility for the broken tie. One is not bound to chase after the unbelieving partner if he or she leaves, for the separation is not of the believer's making.

The question still persists, however, as to whether this separation constitutes divorce. Although many have tried to equate the word "depart" (*koridzetai*) with divorce, the conclusion cannot be drawn from the grammar. The thirteen usages of the term in the New Testament indicate it simply means "to depart" or separate.

It should be recognized, however, that other relations accompanying the desertion may give proper grounds for divorce. If sexual immorality is engaged in or if the desertion is so prolonged as to give no prospect of reconciliation, a *de facto* divorce will have taken place, whether or not it has been sought or granted. The general length of time recognized by many churches to indicate a permanent desertion has been one year. Such a period would indicate either the partner's death, his or her living in immorality, or his or her refusal to fulfill the marriage vows. Since the Bible does recognize divorce as permissible and necessary at times, such a time period would certainly give ample evidence of the deserter's unfaithfulness, unless there are other mitigating circumstances to suggest otherwise. Although God's desire is always for reconciliation, where that is impossible because of the partner's recalcitrance, there is no useful purpose served in refusing to acknowledge dissolution. Desertion in that sense becomes divorce.

Summation. The principle that God hates divorce is emphasized equally in both the Old Testament and the New Testament. That divine principle has never changed, for such a breakup aborts the basic purposes for which God has put man and woman together in intimate relations. However, when the basic physical relationship has been violated by sexual unfaithfulness, the one-flesh union is *de facto* dead. A triangular situation is especially abhorrent to God, as noted by Christ and Paul. Where it was engaged in during Old Testament times, it was the result of being out of the will of God and condoned by Him only as a temporary concession. The first triangle is seen to come in the wicked line of Cain, who also introduced murder. God never endorsed the practice and no good ever came of it, even in the line of the godly.

When divorce does take place because of a partner's unfaithfulness, remarriage should not be the immediate recourse of the believer. Those who have tasted the grace of God in salvation should first be concerned with the restoration of their fallen partner. This is the first concern of God and should be also of the partner sinned against. The sin of unfaithfulness, after all, was primarily against God. To effect such a reconciliation, God has provided an adequate array of spiritual resources which are to be appropriated.

The situation, however, may have gone beyond the point of reconciliation. When such reconciliation has been made impossible because of a new marriage union by the departing spouse, the former union is then to be recognized as completely dissolved. Though divorce is contrary to the will of God, when it is perpetrated by a self-willed individual, the Almighty acknowledges the dissolution just as He also recognizes other sins and their consequences. The consequences must then be faced by both parties, and that brings us to an inevitable question in the aftermath. That question concerns the forthcoming subject of the propriety of remarriage after divorce.

4
The Believer's Right to Remarry

The issue of divorce is only half the problem in a marriage breakup. Consideration of remarriage inevitably follows. In the United States it is more likely that divorced people in any age group will remarry than it is that those who have never married will marry. One fourth of the persons who marry today have been divorced (*An Open Book to the Christian Divorcees*, Roger H. Crook, p. 138). The urge to merge is somehow not lessened by a bad previous experience. Whatever may have been the cause of the breakup, divorced people usually try it again with someone else within two or three years.

This desire for a retry in a second match is certainly not limited to unbelievers. The loneliness and trauma of marital separation affects the constitution of any individual. As often testified, to be divorced is to lose a part of yourself, regardless how intolerable the former union was, and the gnawing desire for a fulfilled union is often even more pronounced after divorce. Although religious convictions may dictate against it, the need and desire are not shrugged off by those convictions. The loss of companionship and the need for sympathetic understanding tend to heighten the desire to give the marriage game a rerun. And with remarriage more socially acceptable today, believers are increasingly joining those who remarry after divorce.

The Need for a Biblical View

What does the Bible say about remarriage? Although many divorced people do remarry, the haunting question often remains as to the propriety of the new union. Is remarriage really a biblical option for believers, or does the second round constitute living in adultery while the previous mate is still living? Recognizing that the Bible does see divorce as permissible and at times necessary, our further question is whether it allows remarriage after divorce. If it does, can one be sure of God's full blessing on the second venture? This is a gray area for many who have been caught between their natural passions, family responsibilities, and a nagging conscience. Not really sure of what the Bible says on the question, they are forced to play it by ear, so to speak, hoping they will be forgiven for their ignorance.

Many opinions, of course, have been expressed as to the propriety of remarriage, ranging from the strongly ascetic traditional view to the more liberal, compassionate view that lets "your conscience be your guide." With the snowballing of the problem today, the trend is admittedly toward the "redemptive" emphasis of liberal compassion, rather than the more stringent traditional position. The gospel's "start over" concept is increasingly being extended to the home as a more realistic approach than the traditional no-remarriage view. Thus an apparent open-mindedness is prevailing with respect to tradition and the conscience in grappling with the issue. Neither tradition nor conscience, however, gives one the solid assurance that is needed for such a crucial decision. When the going gets tough in the down-to-earth aftermath of that decision, the remarried or single person is in need of some divine authority, rather than mere sentimental opinion. Therefore, it is essential to lay hold of the biblical passages and the principles that were given for just such hard decisions of life. Let's put together the various passages that deal with the question of remarriage.

The Right to Remarry

The Bible's allowance for remarriage. It should first be recognized that remarriage itself is not a sin. It was allowed and even required at times under the Mosaic law and was not challenged by Jesus when He was questioned on it (Matt. 22:23ff.). We should remember that God designed marriage as an institution for this life, not for the life to come (Matt. 22:30). There are no human marriages that carry on into the eternal state. Thus, when one partner dies, the other is perfectly free to remarry in the will of God (Rom. 7:2,3; 1 Cor. 7:39). For some, in fact, Paul saw it as essential that they remarry (1 Tim. 5:14). Thus the view that the second marriage is beneath the ideal and somehow God's second best is more sentimental than scriptural. Each union equally points on to the eternal union of Christ and His church.

The biblical ground for remarriage, however, is not limited to those who have lost a partner by death. The Scriptures acknowledge that a marriage partner can be lost in other ways. As previously noted, divorce may do the same thing. The Bible recognizes that when divorce does take place it completely separates a man and wife in their marital union. Though certainly not the ideal, it is none the less the real situation. In the Old Testament the divorced person was forbidden to return to his former union, assuming that marriage to another would take place. This was also the assumption in the New Testament when a marriage was irreparably broken. Let's notice the words of Jesus and Paul as they touched on the subject of remarriage.

The right of remarriage after divorce (Matt. 5:32). Although Jesus referred to divorce on several occasions, He did not speak specifically of remarriage following divorce. The apparent reason is that He simply assumed it when He spoke of divorce. There is no evidence from either the Old Testament or the historical setting of the life of Christ that divorce itself required permanent singlehood for the divided partners. It was generally assumed in that culture that a wife was the "property" of a husband, and to be released by divorce carried with it also the right to be another man's wife (Deut. 24:1,2). This was true in both the Grecian and Roman cultures, as well as that of the Hebrews. The wife could obviously not get an apartment and a secretary's job and single it out on her own, except in most unusual circumstances. She almost had to become the member of another family to survive socially or economically. This usually meant remarriage.

With this in mind, it is easier to understand the omission of the exception clause in Jesus' reference to divorce in Mark and Luke. These accounts simply emphasized His general denunciation of matrimonial breakup which made remarriage necessary. His words were a jolting condemnation to that permissive society where divorce and remarriage were allowed for almost any reason. The wife was at the mercy of the husband's whims, and Jesus denounced this abominable practice of easy divorce. In the Matthew passages, however, the words of Jesus carry with them the strong implication that remarriage followed divorce as a matter of fact. This is especially true in Matthew 5:32 where Jesus declared that "every one who divorces his wife . . . makes her commit adultery" (NASB). Since adultery involves sexual relations with someone else, it is evident that Jesus assumed the divorced wife would marry another. This is overwhelmingly acknowledged by the commentaries on the passage. Remarriage was taken for granted in that culture and we must understand Jesus' treatment of this subject in the light of that setting, not our own traditional setting.

It is evident then that the exceptions that Jesus made in Matthew 5:32 and 19:9 involved both divorce and remarriage. The statement in Matthew 19:9 makes sense only if the exception applies to both parts. Divorce by itself was not adultery, but was considered adultery, since remarriage was assumed as inevitable. If Jesus then acknowledged the propriety of divorce when unfaithfulness took place, He also gave similar acquiescence to the propriety of remarriage in such a case. Though many have in all good conscience tried to limit the exception to divorce, disallowing remarriage, the grammar of Matthew does not sustain that view. The remarriage idea cannot be left out if the logic of His statement is to stand. That pious restriction comes from the asceticism of church history, not from Jesus.

An objection to this understanding of Jesus' words is sometimes made on the basis of John the Baptist's condemnation of Herod in Matthew 14:3,4. In that setting Herod the Idumean king had married his brother Philip's wife, Herodias, which, of course, involved her divorce and remarriage. It should be noted more precisely, however, what John's specific condemnation was. It was not just the divorce and remarriage. He was certainly not suggesting that Herodias should be given back to Philip, for that was contrary to the law of Moses (Deut. 24:1-4). The law did allow divorce and remarriage where certain indecencies took place, but did not allow the rejoining of a couple after an intervening marriage. What John condemned Herod for was rather the sin of marrying his sister-in-law, while his brother still lived. This was specifically condemned by the law as being especially abhorrent to the Lord (Lev. 18:16; 20:21); and the courageous John denounced the king for it before the nation. Had there not been this relationship, the condemnation probably would not have been made against Herod. It would just as aptly have fit the religious leaders, many of whom were of the school of Hillel which allowed permissive divorce and remarriage.

Thus the words of Jesus are not contradicted by those of John the Baptist. They are rather a stinging rebuke against the general practice of divorce and remarriage for any whimsical cause. Jesus specifically distinguished between the proper and improper causes, implying that there are occasions when both divorce and remarriage are allowed in the will of God at the death of a former union.

The right to remarry after desertion (1 Cor. 7). Although Jesus did not speak of remarriage specifically, the apostle Paul did. In his reference to it, however, the apostle dealt with desertion, not adultery, expressing himself strongly against remarriage in such a case (7:11). When a separation has taken place by the desertion of one, the other is not automatically free to marry someone else. Marriages do not dissolve so handily. Paul's counsel, which he describes as from the Lord, was rather that they should remain unmarried or be reconciled. The primary point is that reconciliation of a divided couple is always God's will, not the seeking of a more compatible match.

The following words of Paul (v. 15), however, have often been used to teach that the desertion of an unbelieving partner constitutes complete divorce, and therefore allows the deserted partner the right to remarry someone else. As we previously noted, the words "not under bondage" are taken by many to mean complete freedom from the marriage bond including the right to remarry. They take this divorce of mixed partners to be an exception to Paul's previous counsel to Christian marriage partners. It is thus seen to contravene the previously expressed principles.

66

To this view, however, we are forced to take strong dissent. It is completely gratuitous, opens up an enormous loophole, and is suspect for a number of biblical reasons. First of all, it contradicts the statement of Jesus that God recognizes only one ground for divorce and remarriage, that of the disastrous sin of adultery. The Lord did not appeal to an unreachable ideal standard, but spoke God's word for the workaday world of reality today. He dealt with real situations. In so doing He did not make an exception for the case of mixed marriages of believers and unbelievers, although He addressed the unbelieving Pharisees in Matthew 19. To have made such an exception would have opened the sluicegates to permissive divorce and remarriage.

Second, the view that allows remarriage for mere desertion would be a contradiction to Paul's own words in the context. In 1 Corinthians 7:11-14 he has just counseled separated partners to remain unmarried and to seek reconciliation. If the seeking of a partner's reconciliation is important, how much more important is the seeking of their salvation, if they are unsaved. That is specifically Paul's point in these verses. The unbelieving partner constitutes the believer's mission field, and he is not to give up on that partner simply because the unbeliever runs off. If Paul lived today he would call that a cop-out. It certainly runs counter to the teaching of both Jesus and the apostles on the need for patience, personal sacrifice, and dogged persistence in winning the lost. To close the door on their reconciliation by marrying someone else would be to inoculate them against Christianity forever — a self-serving move at best.

A third reason for rejecting the view that desertion automatically allows remarriage is that the grammatical evidence for it is extremely flimsy. Although the terms "let him leave" and "not under bondage" could grammatically suggest the allowance of remarriage to another spouse, they could also suggest what Paul has just commanded believing partners. That is, don't force an unwilling partner to stay; but if he or she does leave, remain unmarried to wait and work for a reconciliation, and perhaps also their salvation. This grammatical option is certainly more in line with Paul's context, as well as that of the overall New Testament.

If, on the other hand, the partner's desertion is accompanied by or results in their extramarital sexual relations, the case takes on a different complexion. It then falls into the category of adultery and should be treated as such. Though the believer might still want to wait for reconciliation in spite of the deserter's unfaithfulness, they do have the right of remarriage, as acknowledged by Jesus. To wait for their return and repentance is purely an act of grace which may or may not be accorded. If, however, the deserter has remarried or given other evidence that the marriage is beyond reconciliation, that option is out and the privilege of remarriage accompanies the divorce.

This view is also in line with Paul's advice in 1 Corinthians 7:27,28. In saying, "But if you should marry, you have not sinned," the apostle evidently refers to one who has been "released from a wife" (NASB). The term "released" (lelusai) suggests a previous separation, as indicated by the context and Paul's only other usage of the term in Ephesians 2:14. Remarriage in itself is not a sin. The release of which he speaks, however, should not be taken as a mere separation or legal divorce. It should also be taken in the light of Jesus' words that God recognizes divorce only on the grounds of extramarital sex which breaks the union. To overturn Jesus' principle on the subject simply because of Paul's silence and assumption of it is to reject a most basic principle of interpretation. The Scriptures do not contradict themselves, but are always complementary in their progressive revelations. Paul is here acknowledging the right to remarry where a former union is beyond reconciliation. He does not see this remarriage as a concession to carnality, but a legitimate pursuit in the will of God where those conditions exist.

The Need to Remarry

As previously noted, the option of remarriage may not be just a right; it may be a responsibility. It may constitute a physical and spiritual necessity. To see it as a mere right which one may or may not claim falls short of the Bible's overall revelation on marriage and the redemption God provides in Christ. Viewing it simply as a right is to acknowledge one has been wronged and deserves a better break; or that one has failed and grace provides a second chance. That simply emphasizes the punitive aspect and suggests something of a concession. It tends to sap the new marriage of its dignity. It makes it second-class just as the Pharisees saw the sinners of their day. To view our personal salvation from spiritual despair in that way would be to do despite to the redemption God offers. The provision of remarriage must be seen as more than a right to be conceded. It is a positive good to be pursued, when done according to the principles God gave. To see this we should look again at the basic principles for which God has ordained marriage itself. From these we can relate remarriage to the proper fulfilling of several basic needs in a normal human being.

The fulfilling of personal needs. We have previously noted that marriage was designed by God to fulfill many personal needs of a physical, psychological, and social variety. It also has definite spiritual effects. A man or woman is not fulfilled in solitary living. Each one needs the close companionship of a mate who helps to fill him or her out to the God-ordained capacity the Lord intended for that one. If God pronounced it "not good" for Adam, who had not had a mate, to be alone, it is no less so for one who has had one. The death of a partner or even the bad experience of a divorce does not remove that need. It often increases it.

This need follows from the fact that God has so constructed every individual that each has different gifts or capacities. Both Christ and Paul saw celibacy as a gift of God and not necessarily the norm for most (Matt. 19:11,12; 1 Cor. 7:1). Each individual has to determine for himself whether he has this gift by a frank evaluation of his physical and psychological needs. Paul, in fact, cited this human need as one of the reasons for which God ordained the marriage relation (1 Cor. 7:2,9). For this reason he commanded, "let each man have his own wife, and let each woman have her own husband" (v. 2, NASB). Not being a sentimental prude, he recognized the necessity for those without the gift of celibacy to fulfill their God-given sexual needs. For this reason the marriage relation was ordained.

Remembering this basic need and how God placed it there helps us to deal more biblically and realistically with the issue of remarriage. If a person has been married once, it is logical to assume that he or she did not have the gift of celibacy to begin with. Otherwise, he would not have gotten married in the first place. And since he did not have it before, it is pure fantasy to imagine that he suddenly receives this unusual gift of celibacy at the time of divorce (or that he lost the gift of sexual passions). There is no evidence that divorce automatically turns on or off that kind of gift in one's constitutional makeup. It is divinely given and ingrained in the nature of one's being.

This introduces us to a real part of the dilemma in which a divorced person finds himself. As recognized throughout the Bible, the passions of any normal person will cry out for expression. Those passions are to be controlled and only exercised in the God-ordained way — in the marriage relationship. Even in the marriage relationship those passionate desires are at times to be suppressed for certain reasons by mutual agreement (1 Cor. 7:5). Yet, although Paul extolled the single state, he did not advocate it for those without the "gift." The first basic principle that God expressed concerning man was that "It is not good for the man to be alone" (Gen. 2:18, NASB). The divorced person does not all of a sudden become an exception to this rule. He or she is rather thrust into an inner turmoil and conflict within themselves, as well as into an outer frustration and conflict with others.

Paul recognized this turmoil of passions in individuals and saw it as a vulnerable spot for Satan to strike (1 Cor. 7:5). If the adversary works this way in married couples who deprive each other of such fulfillment, how much more would he attack those weakened by the debilitating effects of divorce. The devil is not known for his grace to the weak and susceptible; he is rather more apt to be merciless in moving in for the kill. And the pathetic irony of it is that he often gets so much help from us believers in our pious lack of understanding. A return to Paul's thinking in this regard would indeed be wholesome; it might even be revolutionary. It would really be a return to the sympathy and concern of Jesus as often described in the Gospels. We need to be reminded that the personal needs of a believer in times of disaster are not forgotten by God, and we would do well to take our cue from Him.

The fulfilling of family needs. The casualties of a marriage breakup, however, are not limited to the separated pair. Unfortunately, a family is also usually involved. The children of the breakup thus become the truly innocent parties. At the mercy of circumstances not of their own making, they are thrust into a state of suspense

71

and insecurity at an age when that home security is needed the most. The effects of such a breakup are felt by them in one way or another for life.

Does the Bible reflect this concern for the innocent casualties? I believe that it does throughout its pages. In the light of all that it says about a child's need for a solid foundation of parental love and discipline, we cannot regard it as silent on this aspect of remarriage. The words of Moses and the whole Book of Proverbs, as well as those of Christ and the apostles have a bearing on the issue. Children need parental guidance and that need is not lessened when one parent is lost to them by a divorce. To deny the right or need of remarriage for other reasons of a creedal sort hardly makes compensation to these innocent victims of the disaster. Although God's grace is always sufficient and often overwhelms the disaster of sin, it is not to be presumed upon where alternatives have been provided. We are obligated to discern where God has, in fact, provided such alternatives. To deny such with a mere wave of a theological hand is not only bigoted but also godless. God's remedy for sin is to be sought and followed. If He did indeed pronounce remarriage a sin, it would then be wrong for the bereft partner to seek another mother or father for the children, and God would no doubt provide adequately for that missing link in the home. On the other hand, if the Bible does not see remarriage in such prudish terms, but as sometimes necessary under certain conditions, that avenue of forming a new union and home is God's perfect will. God's provision is always adequate to the need.

The conclusion from this evidence must then be faced. The Bible passages examined show that the Bible does recognize the propriety of remarriage where a disaster has occurred. God does recognize a dissolution where unfaithfulness is involved, and also a new union where that has taken place in good faith. The involvement of children only serves to emphasize that need and to show the divine provision for the innocent victims of the catastrophe where the former union has been dissolved. God provides for little children, but He does it through a father and mother.

As many pastors have experienced, I once was called on to suggest the biblical options for such a case in point. A young girl with two little children had been left by her husband who was living with someone else. They were now divorced and reconciliation was impossible. After a year alone she became acquainted with a young fellow who loved the Lord as well as her and the little tots. Being concerned for the will of God for her life, however, she wanted to know whether a new marriage was proper in the sight of God. With my limited insights at the time, I counseled that it might be the greater sin for her not to marry a proper partner and thereby deprive the small children a father for life. As well as her responsibility to the Lord and herself, she also had a responsibility to provide the children a godly father. From the biblical principles we have examined, I believe today that that counsel was correct. Salvaging the family is definitely a part of the program of our redemptive God.

The Redemption of Remarriage

Remarriage then is definitely a salvage operation in a number of ways. It is admittedly a deviation from the ideal established by God, allowed because of a disaster similar to death. Although it should certainly be seen as a fresh beginning for the two people who see themselves meant by God for each other, there are redemptive factors that must be recognized. It is a new start in the wake of a disastrous failure. To fail to recognize in a realistic way the causes that led to that breakup is to follow the path of failure a second time. The lessons of the failure must be learned to assure success in the new venture.

Redemption begins with repentance. In some ways remarriage is not the same as the first marriage. Although the glory of a new marriage should not be diminished for the new couple, it is a glory that must arise out of failure. Regardless of who the "guilty" party was in the preceding divorce, there was failure on the part of both. For a believer to have a partner fall into sin and unfaithfulness is for both partners to fail to lay hold of the resources God has given for marital success and happiness. That failure must be recognized by both partners involved, and it is futile and irresponsible to simply blame the unfaithful one. That blame must be shared and confessed to God. I do not believe it necessarily should be proclaimed to a congregation any more than other private sins need to be heralded. But their private confession to God and each other makes the failure a learning process which tends to halt the tendency of its repeating itself in the next union. It should be remembered that the divorce rate for second marriages is reputed to be twice that of first marriages. Like success, failure has a tendency to become habitual. To avoid that, an attitude of repentance toward God and reappraisal of oneself is both necessary and wholesome. That is where personal salvation begins, and it is also the starting place for marital salvation in the second try.

As believers contemplate marriage after a dissolution, it is especially vital that they consider only one who is a believer. This is true for all marriages of believers, of course (1 Cor. 7:39), but needs special stress in remarriage. The loss of a marriage partner makes one vulnerable to subjective tendencies, since it often results in the transfer of affections quickly. This is so for the various reasons previously noted. Needs have been unmet and the vacuum of unfulfillment becomes more pronounced. In this situation it is easy to overlook spiritual qualifications, seeking rather the fulfillment of those needs not previously met. A good provider or loving mate, for instance, might appear qualifications enough, with the hope of winning that one to Christ later. Such a venture, however, is out of the will of God and makes for another divided home. It really gives little prospect for the new mate's salvation. Only remarriage to another believer can be redemptive and start with the claim of God's blessing on the union.

Remarriage constitutes a new life. Having repented of the past and learned its lessons, the former union is then to be forgotten in the sense that it is forgiven by God. In the analogy of personal salvation, the old life is to be put away. A distraught couple once came to me with the conviction that they were "living in sin" because one partner had been previously married. They were told that they were now living in adultery. Their concern was whether they should, according to the Bible, be divorced so that the old marriage could be resumed. Or, how were they to right the wrong according to the will of God? A little thought made it obvious that the previous marriage could not be resumed and would even be contrary to Moses' law if it were (Deut. 24:1-4). How were they then to rectify their past and be assured of living in the will of God? The answer is that they should simply recognize the sin that was involved, repent of it toward God, and resolve with God's help to build a successful Christian home together. Scrambled eggs cannot be unscrambled but the couple that remarried can be rededicated as they are to God.

Remarriage then is to be regarded as a new life and redemptive experience. It is not to be lived with compunctions of guilt and a haunted conscience of regrets, but to be accepted as a new experience in the perfect will of God. God's concern after their repentance has taken place is that the new couple pick up the pieces, put it all together with

75

divine help, and move on from there. This was doubtless part of the mission of Jesus as He visited the home of the Samaritan woman for two days in John 4, for only the one she then lived with could have become her husband. The Lord is in the salvaging business, and the rebuilding of half-destroyed homes is part of that program. It is essential that we recognize this redemptive aspect of remarriage and never underestimate the grace and power of God in this home-reconstruction business. And if it is His business, it ought to be ours.

5
The Question of Christian Service After Divorce

The question inevitably arises as to how divorced people can properly serve the Lord. Are they castaways as far as Christian service is concerned? Is divorce an indelible blight on their lives as related to the church and its public service? Having found a new sense of marital fulfillment, the remarried couple often is relegated to the inactive grandstands, except for supporting the work with their tithes and offerings. If that policy is to be continued, we should be sure of its biblical base, for it has far-reaching implications for the church today. What are the biblical limitations for those who have come through the tragedy of marriage breakup?

We should first of all remember that Christian service for believers is not an option; it is an opportunity given as a command (Matt. 28:18-20; Acts 1:8). We are saved to serve. We serve to grow and reflect the glory of God so that others will also be drawn to Him (Matt. 5:16). God has a job to do in this world and He wants His children to be workers together with Him (1 Cor. 3:9). For this reason He has equipped each one with spiritual gifts and has provided the spiritual power to be effective in their use. When the believer's work is done God calls him home to heaven. The Bible knows of no retirement for believers before that

77

homeward call, for when we become weak, we really get stronger in His strength (2 Cor. 12:10). Though the assignments may change, the responsibility for service continues.

When considering the problem of divorce and remarriage, it is important to keep this responsibility of each believer in mind. Several passages of Scripture do touch on the marriage qualifications for church leaders, and therefore the place of divorcees in Christian service has been greatly disputed. What are the limitations meant by those passages? Does Paul rule the remarrieds out of leadership positions in the church? If so, what are their proper roles in Christian service? Furthermore, how should they use the gifts God has given them with the assurance of God's blessing, or are their leadership gifts turned off by their past marital problems? Does the tragedy of divorce constitute them "second-class" church members, disqualified from leadership roles?

These are some tough but crucial questions especially for our day, and they need forthright, scriptural answers. They affect not only an increasingly large group of individuals coming into the church, but also the effectiveness of the church as a whole. Since Christian service is a work of faith, we must know the potential of each of our members. To be effective in the work of faith, we also need the assurance of God's blessing on that service without any twinges of doubt as to the propriety of it. David couldn't have attacked Goliath if he had been unsure of God's presence and power with him. Likewise, we need to allay our doubts on this issue and find the assurance of faith to undergird us. To do this we are again driven to our one source of authority, the Bible. Reflecting on church creeds and scholarly opinions certainly is useful, but we cannot build upon them. Faith needs a "Thus saith the Lord" on which to stand. Let us then take a fresh look at the pertinent Bible passages and relate them to the principles we have already reviewed.

The Bible's Qualifications for Church Leaders

God allows anyone to be saved, but only on His conditions. Likewise, He allows every believer to serve, but only on His conditions. We do not serve, for example, by exalting ourselves, with selfish motives, or in the energy of the flesh. We serve by the rules of the game He has established. It is His "ball game," to use the idiom of our day. While this is true for all believers, it is especially true for those whom He has appointed as church leaders. He has a definite standard of qualifications. In assigning these qualifications for leaders, however, God was not capricious or unreasonable. He gave them with a logical design in view. Seeing God's rationale in establishing those qualifications will help us to appreciate their purposes and to relate them to the issue at hand.

God's rationale in setting standards for leaders. The central passage on the qualifications for church leaders is 1 Timothy 3. Titus 1 also elaborates on the qualifications for elders, but Paul does not there deal with deacons. The qualities of those chosen to serve in Acts 6 should also be noted, since they were chosen with a view to service and leadership. They were selected "to deacon" (*diakonein*), that is, to serve (Acts 6:2). These constitute our basic scriptural sources.

In examining these various passages and their contexts, we discover the reason certain standards were set up for church leaders. It was not to form an elite group of "holy Joes" or to devise a means of rewarding the good guys. Nor was it to organize a corps of clerical "generals" to outrank and command the ecclesiastical troops. Certainly it was not to separate those who served Christ from those who did not. All believers are called to serve. Rather, its purpose was to form a standard for those who would be examples to the flock and good representatives of the church to the world. The church is Christ's instrument in the world today, and He is particular about who leads it. He wants its special representatives to be a good testimony in the world and a proper reflection of His character. He commissions all believers to serve, but not all to lead. Hence His standard of excellence for leaders.

The central characteristic of church leaders. Recognizing God's purpose in establishing leadership standards makes it easier to see His central concern. That central concern in choosing church leaders is spiritual maturity. This is evident in all three passages that discuss these qualifications. Especially is this apparent in 1 Timothy 3, where Paul gives the necessary qualifications for the various groups that serve. The general requirements listed are those of good moral character, good domestic relations, respectable social relations, a proper sense of spiritual priorities, and a sober and mature view of life. For elders or pastors he added the qualities of teaching and leadership abilities.

It thus is evident that Paul emphasized the centrality of good character in all the relationships of church leaders. More specifically, that emphasis was on present character or spiritual maturity, rather than on their past. He mentions nothing of their pedigree, past attainments in the business or religious world, nothing of their moral background out of which they came, or even of their talents and education. In warning against novices he does suggest the need for a proving period, but primarily to demonstrate their present godly character. Their spiritual stability is the main issue.

The reason for this emphasis is given in 1 Timothy 3:14-16. Paul's concern was that the leaders might be examples of godly character and behavior in the church.

They are to lead the flock by their commendable character and biblical teaching. Thus he detailed these qualifications for leaders so that the church members should "know how one ought to conduct himself in the household of God, which is the church of the living God, the pillar and support of the truth" (1 Tim. 3:15, NASB). In the following verse, Paul then elaborates on this purpose by describing one of the reasons Jesus was manifest in human form; it was to give us a revelation of holy and proper conduct in the world. The Lord wants His special representatives in the church to be demonstrations of His character to both the church and the world. Their godly character is His central concern.

The marital status of church leaders. One of the initial qualifications for elders mentioned by Paul in both 1 Timothy and Titus concerned their marital status. He also included it as one of the final qualifications for deacons in 1 Timothy 3:12, though it is not mentioned in Acts 6:3-5. Thus the marriage status was considered a major issue in the choice of both elders and deacons. It has a special bearing on their character and testimony. What precisely was that qualification?

The phrase that Paul used in setting this standard was a "one-wife-man" or husband (*mias gunaikos anayr*; 1 Tim. 3:2,12; Titus 1:6). This qualifying term was preceded in the standard for elders by the requirement that they be blameless or above reproach. The condition of a proper marital status thus appears to flow naturally and essentially from the initial qualification of being "blameless." Though these standards were not mentioned in either Jesus' choice of the Twelve or the church's selection of Matthias in Acts 1:21ff., they were doubtless assumed in view of the qualifications given here by Paul.

The question at issue then is what is meant by a "one-wife-man." Is he one who has been married at least

81

once, to at least one, only once, once at a time, or what? Many views have been espoused throughout church history for a variety of reasons. Several of these views may be ruled out to begin with as lacking support or being contrary to other Scriptures. The Greek Catholic view that marriage is required of leaders can hardly be the point, since Paul himself was unmarried (1 Cor. 7 and 9:5), as was the Lord. The exception of the person having the gift of celibacy has already been noted. The Mormon view of "at least one" involves serious grammatical manipulations and is certainly contrary to the rest of the New Testament. The emphasis is not on a "wife-man," but a "one-wife" man.

It is also unlikely that Paul militates against one who has remarried after the death of his first wife. He has already acknowledged the propriety of such a remarriage for a woman, and doubtless assumes this for a man as well (Rom. 7:2,3; 1 Cor. 7:39). The propriety of this is never questioned throughout the Bible, except on some other basis. Finally, it is doubtful that Paul merely set the standard of being married to "only one at a time" (A. T. Robertson, Word Pictures, IV, p. 572). Polygamy was generally outlawed in the empire of that time and would hardly be a lofty standard needing insistence by Paul. Bigamy was considered adultery for all believers and would be assumed as a disqualification for leadership without mention. How then should we understand Paul's requirement that church leaders be "one-wife-men"?

We should first of all recognize that Paul wrote with a full understanding of Jesus' principle that only monogamy is God-ordained. He always built on the principles that Jesus had already laid down, never contrary to them. Therefore, we should seek to understand Paul in the light of Jesus and the original principles He stressed from the Old Testament. In this light the "one-wife-man" is one

82

who has a character of marital stability. He is not necessarily one who has actually been married, for he may have the gift of celibacy. Certainly such a gift does not restrict one from church leadership, as previously noted about Paul. Neither is he one who has a history of being married only once, for a former wife may have died. Rather, he is one who is faithful in his marital relations, not having wandering affections for the opposite sex. By this qualification Paul is careful to restrict the sexually unstable from the office of pastor and deacon. Such deviants are not a good testimony to the church or the world of dedication to the will of God. Instability here shows noncontrol of the passions, and one who cannot rule himself cannot lead God's people.

The question of character or history. In further evaluating this "one-wife" quality as it relates to the other qualifications given by Paul, it is evident that he is speaking more of one's *character* than of his *history.* Though a person's history obviously tells much of his character, that is not Paul's central concern here. One's past history may not necessarily portray his present character. It is possible to have a good marital history of a single marriage and have a "cat-calling" character of wandering affections at the same time. On the other hand, it is also possible to have a sorrowful marital history of a broken marriage while having a personal character that is above reproach. The tragedy may not have been of his own making, as noted with the prophet Hosea. It therefore is doubtful that Paul is prescribing in this qualification a merely pharisaical standard of outward conformity to a rigid rule. His concern is rather for character and spiritual maturity as demonstrated in the crucial area of one's relations with the opposite sex. He must be a person with his sexual passions under control as he tends and leads the flock of God.

We come then to the problem of whether a divorced

man should be allowed to serve as pastor or deacon. If divorce restricts one from the pastorate, it also restricts one from being a deacon, for the biblical qualification is the same for each. This makes the issue more sensitive, but it forces us to a more balanced and realistic approach from the biblical viewpoint.

Before noting the biblical conclusion on the matter, I must confess that I, personally, have usually been less than candid with the Bible data, and probably more swayed by traditional prejudices in my approach to it. And, like myself, many conservatives have felt that divorce is a stigma on one's life that approaches the character of the cardinal sins, from which there is never release to full Christian service. Many churches, for instance, do not allow a divorced person to be either a deacon or deaconess, regardless of how that divorce came about. In reflecting on this, the implications are staggering. The truth is that God Himself could not be a deacon in most of our churches, let alone the pastor, without getting a special waiver. The Lord, you will recall, had a divorce. The Book of Hosea, as we have noted, outlines the Lord's court charges against the nation Israel, indicating His plan to divorce her for unfaithfulness. In Jeremiah 3:8 the southern prophet tells us that the Lord went through with that divorce from the northern kingdom. Certainly He continues to extend His grace to her and will one day win her back in remarriage, as did Hosea with Gomer. But a divorce was incurred because of the unfaithfulness of the chosen nation Israel. (This earthly union of Jehovah the triune God, by the way, should not be confused with the heavenly, eternal union of Christ with His church.) That temporary divorce of Jehovah, was, of course, the result of Israel's unfaithfulness, not the Lord's. There was an "innocent party" in that case, whether we would allow it for others or not. It was the Lord who made this analogy, not some commentary.

84

Furthermore, there is also an inevitable inconsistency and arbitrariness in denying leadership roles from those who have experienced the tragedy of divorce. How far should those restrictions on the divorced be carried? If they cannot be a deacon or a teacher, can they be an usher? Would a testimony be allowed? If so, would that testimony be allowed to be given from the pulpit? Would they also be allowed to include the reading of a Scripture passage, or would this be preaching? To press it further, would the divorced be permitted to sing in the choir? How about a solo? Or would such performance border too closely to the concept of ministry? Perhaps the distinction might be made that they be permitted to minister with their hands, but not with their voices. I have not heard of any churches that restrict the divorced from contributing to the offering plate. In reflecting on these problems, the inconsistencies begin to abound.

The truth becomes apparent that such restrictions often deny these individuals the service Christ commanded for them in the Great Commission. They tend to atrophy their God-given talents for service and, in fact, restrict the church itself from developing its full redemptive potential. Though the restrictions are well-meant in the interest of preserving purity and discipline for service, they often turn out to be hamstrings that cripple rather than exercises that strengthen. Severity, it should be remembered, is not necessarily the key to effectiveness, as such, except as it relates to the commands of the Word. The Roman Church's requirement of celibacy for the priesthood is a case in point. In its development the Fathers argued that if being married only once indicated purity and dedication, not being married at all was stricter still and therefore more meritorious. This strict celibate view they developed contrary to the analogy of the Old Testament priesthood, as well as the words of Christ and the apostles. Stranger still, their patron apostle Peter was the one apostle the Gospels single out as being married. By their standard, Peter himself couldn't be a priest, let alone pope. The point is that severity is not the issue in setting qualifications for church leaders. Asceticism is not necessarily holiness. It may represent mere pharisaical pride and will-worship. On the contrary, the key to effectiveness and God's blessing in the ministry is discovering precisely what God declares in the Bible and applying His Word and principles to the ministry.

How then should we apply the "one-wife" qualification to our choosing pastors and deacons? As previously noted, we are obligated to understand Paul's qualifications in line with Jesus' teaching and principles on the matter of divorce. Jesus clearly acknowledged that, although divorce and remarriage are contrary to God's original plan for man, it can indeed happen through sin. Where a former spouse has been unfaithful and has remarried another, Jesus saw divorce and remarriage as inevitable for the bereft partner (as noted in Matt. 5 and 19). Denouncing this inevitable consequence of the tragedy was not the point of Jesus' condemnation, but the danger of fornication itself. The fact is that remarriage following such a debacle accompanied with proper repentance is never denounced elsewhere in the New Testament, and it is extremely doubtful that Paul set up a standard above or contrary to that of Jesus. As noted in the previous chapter, God does recognize such a divorce and remarriage where the death of a former union has taken place, which allows for the fulfilling of His will in the personal and family needs of the partner left. And Paul is not here starting the Nicolaitan heresy by prescribing a legal plane of super-virtuosity for the clergy or diaconate, unreachable for the flock they seek to lead. He is rather simply building on Jesus' principles and emphasizing again the need for church leaders to be

chosen in line with Jesus' insistence on marital faithfulness.

This brings us again to Paul's primary emphasis on
character and relates the "one-wife" qualification to this
emphasis. His concern is for the leader's present character
and moral maturity as related to the opposite sex. Is this
then a lowering of standards that opens the doors to lax
morals and permissiveness? The opposite is true. It puts
the emphasis where Jesus put it, on the heart and present
character, rather than on an outward record of a marital
history. The emphasis is not so much on what a man once
was as it is on what he now is. His previous life of sin
before salvation, for instance, should have no bearing, for
that was another life. The Corinthian believers, as Paul
declared, were saved out of sexually depraved corruption,
but that had no apparent limitations on their service and
their gifts of ministry (1 Cor. 6:9-11). The all-important
point is the leader's personal character.

In dealing with the flock, then, the church leaders
must have a marital stability that is unswerving. Wavering
here can be catastrophic. The pastor must be able to counsel and deal with the women of his flock without being
sexually affected by his own uncontrolled passions. This
does not mean that he should wear blinders when around
the opposite sex or look the other way when the young
beauties walk by. If he is sexually distracted in this way, he
is not really fit for Christian service. Rather, he should be
so single-minded in his marital relations at home and so
controlled in his passions that he can minister to the spiritual concerns of both sexes without becoming sexually
involved in either his thoughts or actions. This is the
standard Jesus set for every believer (Matt. 5:28), but it is
especially essential for those who lead. The pity is that
such a sexual mind-set is not sufficiently emphasized as a
basic prerequisite for service, and the devil has played

enormous havoc in this area. Any pastor, deacon, or church leader with untamed, wandering affections would do the church a favor by leaving his office, rather than remaining in it to feed his ego and passions. Purity comes between pardon and power, and that purity must start with the leaders. The church would go further faster with fewer if this qualification of singleness in marital affections were emphasized as absolutely essential in the thought and character of its leaders. That was undoubtedly the point of Paul as he insisted that the church's leaders be "one-wife-men."

This forces us to a reevaluation of the place of remarried people in the ministry of the church. The crucial issue is not their history, but their character; not their past, but their present. Their history is indeed important where it reveals impenitence and an unwillingness to acknowledge their failure in a marriage breakup. Such have not learned the lesson of their failure and will only propagate that failure in others. Where such repentance and confession have not occurred accompanied by a change in character and spiritual stability, they definitely are not qualified to represent the church in public service. Where this change has taken place, however, that person's qualifications and character should be evaluated in the light of that change. God is able to use an unfaithful apostle Peter after restoration to reach out with sympathy to other unfaithful people. He delights to salvage broken things and put them into productive service. He did that with murderous Saul of Tarsus, adulterous Augustine, and Mary Magdalene, to mention but a few outstanding examples. Salvaging personalities and homes is His specialty.

It often is conceded that one's marital status before salvation should not be an issue, but only his marital history after being saved. A divorce following salvation, according to this view, restricts one from church leadership positions. We should note, however, that the question is not that cut and dried. Spiritual maturity does not automatically come at the point of conversion, but often is a gradual process. Therefore, to arbitrarily set that as the point from which marital stability must be measured is to fall again into the legalistic trap of merit building by outward conformity. To fail to immediately grow by stumbling in the marital area is thus to cut one's self off forever from the exercise of certain spiritual gifts in the church. That the Bible sets that probationary period is hard to defend.

The real issue in Paul's qualifications rather concerns one's present moral character and spiritual maturity. And these must be evaluated in the light of how God's redemptive grace has been appropriated as the individual is now related to God and man. The blessing Jesus promised was to the "pure in heart," not necessarily the pure in history. It is through such individuals that He pours His blessing of redemptive grace, and we can ill afford to shut off any such channel through which God has chosen to work. Some of His greatest trophies of grace are redeemed and reconstituted homes, the members of which are vibrant and thankful testimonies of that grace. To stifle that testimony at the church level smacks more of Pharisaism than of the redemptive grace and power of God. The command to serve is given to both redeemed individuals and redeemed homes.

6
God's Matrimonial Principles Summarized

There are some things that admittedly defy analysis and romance is usually classed in that category. How do you describe dimples, for instance, without destroying their romantic attraction? The Bible's description of true romance, however, is not just a twinkle of the eye or a nebulous feeling of the heart that dissolves by description. It is a carefully planned experience of both the heart and head and is designed to be governed by a number of guiding principles. If it is a "game" we play, it was God who introduced it, and He also provided a set of "rules" by which the game is to be properly and enjoyably played. Let's summarize those rules in terms of broad, guiding principles.

In reviewing these principles, we should remember that they are designed primarily for those who are believers and have accepted the Bible as their guide for life. Though unbelievers may profit in some ways by recognizing these principles, such people are really outside the family of God and operate on standards other than those of the Bible. The marital counsel God gives is for His own family. He has no offer of "domestic salvation" for those who refuse His offer of personal salvation. They are "on their own," so to speak, for the biblical counsel on marriage is for those who have made Christ the Lord of their lives.

It should be noted furthermore that the Bible does not present a variety of different and conflicting standards for different ages. There is a basic consistency running through the Old and New Testaments on the issue of marriage. God's standards do not change from one dispensation or generation to another. He is the same yesterday, today, and forever, as to His essence and principles. Although He has revealed His will throughout the Bible in a gradual and progressive way to people of different cultures and levels of maturity, His basic principles with men are always the same. He does not change His ideals. Though He does not correct all imperfections in their elementary stages, His ultimate goals are not self-contradictory. This is important to keep in mind as we seek to harmonize the various contributions made throughout the Bible on the subject. When we recognize that each one complements or builds on the other, a unique consistency is discovered throughout with respect to the divine principles of marriage.

Recognize the Real Purpose of Marriage

In summarizing the principles, we shall move from the normal to abnormal situations. The first essential in any game is to know its purpose, and that certainly applies to marriage. To miss the purpose is to lose the game or not to recognize when you have won. Although a number of purposes for marriage have been noted in the Bible, the most basic is that of personality building. That building is not just of our children, but also of ourselves. God is in the business of salvaging and transforming human personalities, and the marriage relation is one of His primary workshops. Here human relations rub the closest and personality growth is put to its keenest test. When we recognize that all believers are meant to grow, and that growth comes through struggle, it is not surprising that the home often becomes the arena for some of that struggle. As the two partners relate in various ways, the differences and problems that arise should not be seen as unusual or deplorable in themselves. Those problems or personality clashes are really designed to drive the couple to the Word of God for His wisdom and strength to further mellow and mature them into the likeness of God. The struggles should be seen as those of a workshop, not of a fighting "ring" (the wedding band is not meant to signify that kind of a ring). In this workshop we are workers together with God in His work of fashioning personalities for eternity.

Marriage then was ordained by God as one of man's highest institutions. Although the propriety of being single is not questioned, the single state is not the norm, but an exception in the general plan of God (Gen. 2:18). Each individual is to discover God's will in this regard for himself. This is determined by recognizing the "gift" God has given to him or her in terms of their sexual passions. Paul strongly advised that one's passions are to be listened to as the individual makes this decision of whether to marry or not to marry for himself (1 Cor. 7:2,9). The apostle was an outstanding example of one with the gift of celibacy who could grow spiritually without the marriage relationship. Most of us, however, do not have that divinely given gift. Paul himself recognized this, having perhaps learned it from Jesus' words (Matt. 19:11,12). Most of us need the gift of a partner to help us develop into our full potential for God. In this relationship we also typify the eternal union of Christ and His church which will be the epitome of bliss and personal fellowship. Remembering this divine relationship also serves to enhance the human relationship of the partners. We are building each other up for eternity.

Recognize God's Resources in Times of Marital Stress

In spite of our best intentions, however, times of stress inevitably arise. The "rose garden" is apt to lose its petals and sweet aroma at times, and only the thorns seem to stand out. What is a believing couple to make of this? Does this suggest that they may have been out of God's will in choosing each other and now are being chastised? Did they make a "bum choice" after all and henceforth are doomed to incompatible living?

At such times it should first be recognized that their being married to each other was and is the perfect will of God. That will should never be questioned. Even if they were out of God's will when getting married, it is always God's will that they remain married once they are. Their problem is not the wrong choice in the past, but the failure to lay hold of God's resources in the present. No couple is entirely compatible to begin with, so let's forget the incompatibility bit. Grappling with incompatibilities is part of the challenge God has given for spiritual living. Whatever the problem or difference, the Lord has the resources available to turn human incompatibilities into divine compatibilities. Laying hold of that divine resource and aid will enhance the relationship, building a stronger bond of three cords.

In seeking to utilize this resource, each of the partners should recognize their God-given responsibilities to each other. These we have called self-evaluation and spouse-evaluation. Self-evaluation must come first on the part of the concerned partner. This self-appraisal is designed to evoke a similar self-evaluation on the part of the other partner, if we make the application in sincerity. The showing of love, concern, patience, helpfulness, submission, cheerfulness, and other relational virtues has a way of reproducing the same in others. With such an attitude, spouse-evaluation also becomes more objective, being

94

done in a different spirit. Thus self-evaluation becomes the soil for productive spouse-evaluation, which in turn results in personality growth for both partners.

In this pursuit, however, it should be recognized that a response in the other person does not always occur automatically in the sense that you just push the right "spiritual button." People are not automotons. No two people have the same degree of spiritual or personal maturity and no two respond exactly the same way. Growth of any kind is a gradual and progressive process. However, the divine resources are available to bring about the proper responses at the right time. Those spiritual resources are the Word of God, an example of godly living, and prayer. To utilize these resources is to move the hand of God who is capable of handling any situation. He especially delights to work with these kinds of problems, for the home or family is His favorite area of operation. He will move heaven and earth if necessary to resolve the marital differences and will, in the process, impart His own nature into the marriage partners' personalities. But He needs someone to invite Him to come in with the "tools of His trade." With those tools of the Word and prayer He can reconcile or renovate any marital situation.

Recognize God's Recourse in the Event of Marital Breakup

There are times, however, when the divine resources have been forgotten or neglected, and marital breakup takes place, even with Christian couples. Having the right medicine or principles is of no avail if they are not used. In that case, God allows nature to take its course, even to the point of breakup or unfaithfulness. What counsel does the Bible give for such a situation?

At such times it is essential to remember that God has but one path to follow. His one will for a marriage breakup is that reconciliation take place. Whether separation or divorce has taken place, His one desire for the couple is that they be reconciled. He leaves us no options to this plan. This road to recovery should begin with repentance toward God and a spirit of repentance and reconciliation toward each other. It is futile for the so-called "spiritual" partner to place all the blame on the other, for breakups are rarely one-sided. Aside from the outward symptoms, both are inwardly guilty of not employing the spiritual resources God has provided. Reconciliation then must start with the repentance of both partners. As repentance is the turning point in personal salvation, so it is also the turning point in domestic salvation. The resources of the Word, prayer, and a submissive and flexible spirit are then to be brought into play to invoke God's help in bringing about that reconciliation. Reconciliation is always God's will, for He hates divorce (Mal. 2:16).

When unfaithfulness or adultery has taken place on the part of one of the partners, however, the problem then takes on a different complexion. The tragic sin of extramarital sex is so devastating in God's eyes as to signify the death of the marriage. The permissive attitude of our "gay" age is entirely foreign to the Bible. Both Jesus and Paul stressed the enormity of the crime of marital unfaithfulness, as already emphasized throughout the Old Testament. No Bible writer ever suggested a compromise in this regard. Fornication is the one cause Jesus recognized as legitimate grounds for divorce (Matt. 5:32; 19:9). Paul, in fact, saw it as tantamount to marriage to the harlot (fornicator; 1 Cor. 6:16). Where such infidelity has taken place, then, it is a call for separation or for bringing the issue to a head. God does not tolerate such immoral relations, and the other partner is likewise not to put up with it. Allowing it to continue without confronting it is to condone what God hates. The law is to be laid down with righteous indignation.

Having noted the need for laying down the law, however, we should also remember the counterbalance of grace. Although the words of Jesus give strong evidence that fornication is legitimate grounds for complete divorce, reconciliation is not to be ruled out. For the believer who has tasted of God's forgiving grace, reconciliation with the erring partner should still be sought. Such forgiveness and reconciliation should be extended only on the basis of proper repentance and a sincere reaffirmation of faithfulness to the marriage vows. Without these the reconciliation is a farce and a prelude to further failure.

The situation, however, may have dissipated beyond repair. It may have gone beyond reconciliation. Although reconciliation is always to be sought as the only option following separation, it may turn out to be an impossibility. Such is the case where the other partner has married another or is living in a common-law situation. When that occurs the former union is permanently broken in God's eyes. This was stressed in the Old Testament as one of the first principles of marital breakup, that a previous union was not to be resumed following a later marriage (Deut. 24:2-4). God called that an "abomination" that pollutes society (Jer. 3:1). When remarriage takes place the bereft partner is to recognize that the former marriage is unalterably broken. Although marriage is a union joined together by God, it can be broken by either of the marriage partners when they persist in pursuing their passions apart from the will of God. The other partner is then to accept that marriage as completely dissolved. He or she is then to begin with repentance to seek the will of God to determine the direction of the new life that lies ahead. There are some things that cannot be changed or unscrambled, but they can be accepted and adapted to. It is essential for such a person to remember that God's will is not permanently lost, but that His perfect will can yet be found by repentance and rededication of his or her life to God.

Recognize the Biblical Place of Remarriage

The question of remarriage after divorce is admittedly one of growing concern for which the church is in dire need of an answer. This is no place for uncertainty, for the lives of an increasing number of couples are involved. The issues and biblical solutions ought to be clear cut. Both the pastor officiating and the partners marrying need this assurance so that the union can be made with a clear conscience or denied with a clear knowledge of God's denial. Such assurance, of course, must come from the Word of God as its principles are seen in a consistent pattern of revelation. If the Bible is our rule of faith and practice, it ought to speak to this gnawing problem of our day. We believe it does.

In varying degrees, two basic views have been taken by the church. The Roman Catholic position summarily disposes with the question by answering it solidly in the negative. Their authority is more papal than biblical, maintaining that marriage is an indissoluble sacrament and therefore divorce and remarriage are out of the question, apart from nullity or death. If we appeal simply to the Scripture, apart from church dogma, however, that sacramental view of indissoluble marriage is difficult to defend. According to Jesus, marriage is not eternal, but for this life, and may be dissolved in the event of fornication. He also recognized that a new marriage might take place following the disaster of a previous marriage being dissolved. As death allows the remaining partner to remarry, so the death of a marriage allows for the same.

This allowance for remarriage was also enunciated by Moses in the Old Testament, and is furthermore elucidated by Paul in 1 Corinthians 7. That means that all who touched on the subject in the Bible held the same, consistent view. They all took a redemptive view of marriage and its breakdown, giving hope for the disrupted partners, regardless at what point the salvaging operation might begin for each partner.

The propriety of remarriage itself. This view of Moses, Jesus, and Paul is further confirmed by several other considerations with respect to the partner that is left. The first concerns the biblical view of remarriage itself. Both the Old and New Testaments recognize the propriety of remarriage after the death of a partner. Marriage itself is not eternal. Paul even suggested the advisability for certain widows to remarry (1 Tim. 5:14). Remarriage is admittedly always wrong while the possibility of reconciliation to the former partner remains. When the former spouse has remarried, however, that possibility is gone forever. That remarriage constitutes adultery and terminates permanently the former union, as though the partner had died. It does not, however, doom the bereft partner to solitary living the rest of his or her life. Neither the Bible nor experience suggest that this course would serve any useful purpose. Rather, remarriage might be the most wholesome for all involved, to forget the past, and might certainly be the will of God when directed by Him to the right person.

The fulfillment of personal needs. The second consideration is the personal needs of the bereft partner. We have noted previously that one of the purposes of marriage is to fulfill many personal needs to promote spiritual growth. One of these needs which the apostle Paul stressed is that of sexual fulfillment (1 Cor. 7:2ff.). This he saw as a spiritual necessity requiring fulfillment to waylay the attacks of Satan. He did not see it as a mere pandering to the carnality of the flesh that should rather be squelched. The exception to this need, of course, is where a person has the gift of celibacy which hardly pertains to divorced persons. People who marry usually do not have that gift. This being so, it is puerile to assume that a person deprived of his or her mate suddenly is endowed with the gift of quieted passions. Such is never suggested in the Scriptures. And if Satan attacks through these unfulfilled needs during marriage, he will surely not lessen those attacks on the one who fights loneliness in the wake of the tragedy of divorce. That need is not portrayed as devilish, but God-given, as noted by both Jesus and Paul. This personal need, it should be remembered, is only one example of a whole array of personal needs that confront the one who is left as the tag end of a dissolved marriage.

The fulfillment of family needs. The third consideration to keep in mind in judging the propriety of remarriage is the family needs of the children that are left. These innocent victims are as much in need of parental guidance as any children, if not more so. In a sense their whole lives are at stake. To deprive them of a father or mother because of some traditional creed from an ascetic age is worse than kidnapping; it is "dad- or mom-napping." They, especially, need the corrective love and discipline of both a mother and dad. God's declaration that "it is not good for the man to be alone" no doubt envisaged also the coming of children who would need that dual influence and guidance. Our own age of increasing crime in conjunction with an increasing number of one-parent homes is a further testimony to this need. That need is everywhere emphasized in the Bible, and it is not diminished by our pious appeal to papal or creedal dogmas of men.

It is thus apparent that these various considerations of personal needs only add impetus to the words of Jesus and Paul on the propriety of remarriage. When a marriage has been terminated and reconciliation is no longer possible, a remarriage is then to be seen as entirely proper in the will

100

of God. It is not to be rushed into but carefully pursued with the lessons of the past clearly in mind. The person seeking God's will after divorce must start with repentance and rededication of his or her life to God. They must be willing to forgive and forget the past with all its misgivings, as they also receive God's forgiveness and erasure of the past. Their choice of a new partner should not be directed by their passions but by the Lord. This is another reason it should not be hurried. Only a believer should be considered and one who is willing to pick up the broken pieces and redemptively build a home for God. It should be the result of time spent with the Lord in spiritual renewal and seeking His counsel for the future.

With this kind of a fresh start, the new couple should have no question but that God will place His blessing on the new home. He is called a Savior because He specializes in salvaging broken lives and families. Compunctions of the past must be put aside. The glory and promise of that new home should not be diminished by past failures, but a new day should be envisioned. Building with God they can build with hope that "maketh not ashamed; because the love of God is shed abroad in our hearts by the Holy Ghost which is given unto us" (Rom. 5:5, KJV).

Recognize the Place of Christian Service Following Divorce

The question of Christian service after divorce is an even stickier one than that of remarriage and the positions are even more entrenched. For many the issue is cut and dried by Paul's requirement that a church leader be "the husband of one wife." Divorced people therefore are eliminated from much Christian service in the church, regardless of how the divorce took place.

The inconsistencies of this position have been discussed and the fact only needs restatement here. Such an across-the-board ruling to a large extent aborts the gifts God has invested in those people and likewise vitiates the commands of Christ for them to serve in proclaiming the gospel. As previously noted, the root of the problem is a misunderstanding of Paul's concept of a "one-wife-man" or woman (1 Tim. 3:2; 5:9; Titus 1:6). The traditional and prevalent view even today is that Paul was speaking of the person's marital history. A little reflection suggests that that is a neat way of setting aside the spirit of the law by meticulously fulfilling the letter, a practice which so nauseated the Lord. To determine its import, we must ask whether Paul was concerned with one's *history* or his *heart* in this qualification. The overwhelming evidence of the context (when we take off our blinders) is that the apostle was primarily concerned with character rather than with history. That is the central thrust of all the passages delineating the qualifications of church leaders. Though the Cretans may have lived lives of corruption in the past, the issue was not their past but their present. The "one-wife-man" qualification insisted on marital stability. It did not require that he be married or married only once. That qualification could be met by many who actually lack a "one-wife" character. As Jesus indicated in the Sermon on the Mount, the main issue is the heart. A church leader must have his sexual passions so controlled that he can effectively minister to both sexes without being distracted by wandering affections. This does not mean that one's marital history is not to be considered, for it often indicates tendencies or character. That history, however, is not to be the determining factor, but his present character and growth in the Lord.

As noted before, this view presents a much higher and more stringent standard than the mere historic idea of being married once. It is really a call for all church leaders to continually check their character in this regard. The central issue in character is the heart which ultimately directs the actions. To relegate this qualification to a mere restriction of divorcees from Christian service is to hush God's siren concerning an ever-growing danger. That it needs emphasis in our day of permissiveness and "loving living" is hardly to be questioned.

The conclusion appears inevitable that Paul was not restricting divorcees from Christian leadership, but he was referring to sexual deviants of all kinds. A leader's marital affections must be single and unswerving. If a person has suffered the experience of divorce, his past should certainly be scrutinized by both himself and the church. The scrutiny may reveal that he has not in fact deviated from his "one-wife" character, though he may not be entirely blameless. Following a time of spiritual renewal in repentance and rededication of his life to God, that "one-wife" character may be reaffirmed or renewed, as might other failing characteristics of leadership. Spiritual leaders are not necessarily those who have made no mistakes, but those who have repented and learned from their mistakes, and, like penitent Peter, have more deeply appropriated the grace and strength of the Lord.

The Redemptive Emphasis of the Biblical Principles

These principles admittedly cut beneath the subterfuge of the traditional slide-rule regulations concerning divorce, remarriage, and Christian service. In this way they also parallel the biblical principles of salvation and Christian growth. Outward conformity and sophistication are not the issue, but inward change is. These principles lay bare and examine the heart. They deal with causes rather than symptoms. They are remedial rather than merely punitive. God's concern is for the home and all those a part of it that each may bloom into his or her full potential of spiritual development and beauty. Where breakdowns occur, He stands ready to restore with His redemptive grace. That remedy involves both discipline and love, but always for the purpose of restoration and further spiritual growth.

I am sure there are many who would reject this redemptive emphasis on the ground that it suggests too easy restoration after a stint in sin. It may appear to promote permissiveness in not consigning all moral deviants to an unpardonable or dormant spiritual state. Such a view, however, fails to recognize both Jesus' point in Matthew 5 and 19 as to the devastating effect of immorality and the uniqueness of God's grace. His grace certainly does not preclude judgment for sin in this life, as we see so vividly portrayed in the sin and punishment of David with Bathsheba. David did receive immediate forgiveness when he repented; but he spent the rest of his life paying for that sin in terms of its consequences in his family. That episode became the "continental divide" of his life between his triumphs and his troubles. His adultery, murder, and deceit turned up time and again in his children and nearly cost him his throne. The effects of that moment of sin were not easily erased by his time of sorrow and restoration to the Lord's fellowship. The record emphasizes that he paid dearly for it. But it should not be forgotten that his deep repentance also brought an enormous display of God's grace in the aftermath. The penitent king became a great testimony through the ages of what God's grace will do. Upon his confession, the Lord promised him a second son by Bathsheba who would become the heir to his throne and the one through whom Messiah would come. That son's name was Solomon, who was specifically appointed to the throne above his older brothers. This story illustrates both the enormity of God's judgment on the sin of immorality and the greatness of his restorative grace where repentance has been genuinely shown.

The point I am making is that God's grace has as its unique feature the ability to overwhelm the disaster of sin and salvage trophies out of tragedies. And the biblical principles by which God can bring restoration and harmony out of marital chaos is an example of that grace. His Saviorhood extends to homes as well as to hearts, and that should be a part of the gospel we preach. He is the wonderful Counselor for broken marriages as well as broken lives, and we are to recognize the completeness of the healing He provides. The imparting of that grace to married couples, we recall, is but a parable of His grace to us who are to be His eternal bride. That coming marriage of Christ and His church should never be lost sight of as we seek to restore and perfect the ideals of human marriage, God's portrait of His grace.

7
The Principles Illustrated
by Typical Cases

We believe that the Bible is our basic source for matrimonial principles. However, the application of these principles is not always illustrated in live situations. Very little, for instance, is said of the apostles' wives and families, and rarely do the writers detail specific marital problems in the early church. This, of course, is typical of New Testament instruction, for the principles were usually given for situations well known to the original readers. Perhaps the Lord did not preserve the details of those situations to prevent our mechanical applications of them. We so easily become slide-rule religionists, cataloging all the problems and solutions in neat formulations. Often their applications are not so mechanically simple.

We have a responsibility, however, to apply the principles to life. These principles for marriage are all-encompassing, as we have seen, and it is our responsibility to understand and apply them with the guidance of the Holy Spirit. To do this it is helpful to see them exemplified in live situations. Illustrations make principles live. Let's review the principles in their chronological order and then see how they apply to some common situations of marital problems today.

The Matrimonial Principles Summarized

Principles for Considering Marriage[1]

1. Marriage was instituted by God and is normally His will for most people.
2. Being single is also God's will for many, and the decision of whether or not a person should marry is an individual judgment for each as he or she evaluates the gifts God has given (with respect to passions).
3. Marriage must be recognized as instituted by God for the personal growth and spiritual development of each. It is not an automatic state of bliss. Differences and incompatibilities that arise should not be seen as insurmountable obstacles, but challenges to spiritual growth as divine guidance is sought.

Principles for Considering Divorce

1. When problems arise, divorce should not be considered as an option, for that was ruled out in the marriage vows. Recourse should rather be to prayer, self-examination, tactful communication, and patient trust.
2. When marriage break-up does occur, reconciliation should always be seen as God's primary desire. A separated couple with spiritual resources should never despair of this happening. Reconciliation should be pursued by the avenue of prayer, with a spirit of humility and forgiveness, and with trust in a God who does the impossible.
3. If unfaithfulness has occurred on the part of one or both, however, the option of divorce is open, especially if that infidelity continues. In the spirit of

---

[1]For scriptural documentation see preceding chapters.

grace, the "innocent" party may opt to simply separate if the sinning partner persists, not seeking divorce while reconciliation is still a possibility.

4. When divorce has occurred and the former spouse has remarried, the situation is completely altered as far as reconciliation is concerned. A new world has to be faced. It is then essential to cultivate a spirit of forgiveness and acceptance of the new circumstance. Bitterness and regrets must be set aside and a fresh reliance on God's will for the future sought. Quick remarriage on the rebound is always dangerous, for it is usually dictated by reactionary impulses. One must guard against a sentimental transfer of affections as the effects of the vacuum are felt.

Principles for Considering Remarriage

1. Remarriage following divorce may be God's will. This should take place only when it is evident that reconciliation with the former partner is no longer possible. It should also follow a time of self-evaluation to learn the lessons of the failure, repentance before God concerning the tragedy, and a period of rededication to God's will.

2. Special care should be given that this second marriage be only in God's will—that is, to one who is a believer and also dedicated to doing God's will. One should beware of uniting with someone who merely satisfies unfulfilled psychological needs in the wake of the past failure.

3. When remarriage in God's will is entered, however, it should be with all the thrill and expectation of a new beginning. It should not be regarded as a second-class experience that God blushes to bless. God's forgiveness is not half-hearted and neither

should our acceptance of it be, but we should fully expect His choice blessing on the new union.

Principles for Christian Service After Marriage Failure

1. Marriage failure inevitably interrupts Christian service. Regardless of who was primarily to blame, the failure carries with it a blotch on one's character and testimony which calls for fresh, personal introspection and a reevaluation of one's relation to God and others. The duration of that interruption depends on the part the individual played in the break-up, the spirit of penitence and humility shown, and the new spirit of dedication to God's service evidenced. The quality of a "one-wife" man or "one-husband" woman must be established. This character quality of marital stability is essential to those in Christian service and it is not developed or reestablished overnight.
2. As all believers are called to fulfill the Great Commission in line with their spiritual gifts, the responsibility extends to those who have suffered marriage failure as well. The type of service depends on their spiritual gifts and the recognition or approval of God's people. Their effectiveness depends on their spiritual, moral, and academic preparation, as God leads each, regardless of their backgrounds.
3. The attitude of the church toward the fallen and reclaimed is all-important. The church is a rehabilitation center, not an incrimination center. A spiritual church will cultivate a spirit of grace toward all its members, whether single, married, divorced, widowed, or remarried. Leadership qualifications should not be determined primarily by one's past history, but by one's present charac-

110

ter. In choosing leaders the concern should be for established character, spiritual gifts, and the evidence of one's dedication to the Lord's service. While the Lord does not tolerate moral looseness, He has shown a remarkable readiness to mend and use broken vessels. It is essential for the whole church that this balance be understood and practiced.

The Matrimonial Principles Illustrated by Case Histories

1. *Is remarriage "living in adultery"*? This question is a common one which concerns the attitude of God toward remarried people. If one or both partners were previously married and divorced, does God see this new relation as an "adulterous" one? If so, should they separate and return to their former partner(s), or how should they resolve the dilemma so that it would be in God's will?

It should first be recognized that the Bible forbids returning to a former mate after remarriage to another has taken place. To do so would incur a second divorce and a second case of adultery. It would be an abomination in the sight of God and would only compound the personal problems of each. "Living in adultery" is not remarriage but living in unfaithfulness to one's marriage partner. When remarriage takes place, any previous marriage is ended forever. It is a point of no return, as far as the previous unions are concerned. The one course of action for a remarried couple is to "pick up the pieces" where they are and move on with an untroubled conscience concerning the past. This is done by acknowledging their past sins and failures, repenting toward God, forgiving all the parties involved, and resolving to build the new home for God. Any pent-up bitterness must be removed to enable the full flow of God's grace. They should then trust God to put His full blessing on the new union. Tragically, many have been haunted by this "living in adultery" delusion after remarriage and have been deprived of God's peace and blessing throughout life because of an ill-informed, hounding conscience.

2. *Should a partner tolerate unfaithfulness?* A young couple was married and in the course of time he was unfaithful to her. Later she became a Christian, but he continued his life of sin and his affairs with other women. Inasmuch as he refused to be counseled or to give up his illicit activities, she sought counsel as to what action she should properly take. Should a Christian partner meekly sit back and tolerate such promiscuity on the part of a mate?

Biblically speaking, that young fellow had repeatedly broken the marriage bond by fornication and was living in an adulterous union. This was a real case of "living in adultery." Such triangular affairs, of course, are an abomination to God. Besides prayer and seeking counsel, the young wife's first responsibility was to extricate herself from the adulterous situation as best she could and refuse to live with the sexual "tomcat." God doesn't tolerate such illicit, barnyard living, and neither should His people. Any further affection she might show him would only tend to approve his actions, not arrest them. That young man sorely needed a shock treatment, and it was her solemn duty to administer it with any help she could get. Their home was already destroyed in God's eyes, and the sooner he was informed, the better. The unrepentant have no claim to God's grace, and it is futile to extend it when God denies it. We are not to tolerate what God abominates. The derelict husband was certainly her mission field, but she was desperately in need of a furlough.

This, by the way, is an increasingly common situation today in many homes outside the church. Some wives are forced to condone it to prevent a break-up and loss of livelihood. Our purpose here is not to serve as a "Dear Abby" column for the world, but the Bible's advice in this regard could well be taken by them as well. Over the long haul, the convenience of board and room with its amenities is not so dear as to be purchased at the price of allowing infidelity to go unchecked.

3. *Should a divorced mother with children remarry?* This question could be enlarged to include all remarriages, but the dilemma is especially acute where children are involved. Let's generalize it. When a mother or father is left with several children after a divorce, does the Bible require that he or she raise them alone rather than remarry? Do the Bible principles make it impossible for these innocent victims of the divorce to have a mother or father throughout life? A large proportion of the divorces involving the young today present this gnawing problem.

There is little doubt that the Lord Jesus envisioned this traumatic situation as He gave instruction concerning the divorce problem. As previously noted, He did not disallow remarriage when the previous union was broken by infidelity. Furthermore, the Bible does not give counsel to single parents on how to be both a father and mother, though such might be inferred. God certainly provides grace for many such dilemmas and does help many bereft partners do the impossible. But that is not normative. Neither in the Old Testament or New Testament is it required that a home should continue with only half of the essential agents that God appointed for its proper order. It rather emphasizes the children's need for love and discipline by both a father and mother. It furthermore emphasizes the personal needs and dangers of the bereft partner who does not have the gift of celibacy. Married people obviously do not have the gift of celibacy, and the God-given gift of passions which they do have must be exercised only in a marriage relation. For these various needs to be fulfilled God has provided the avenue of remarriage when it is evident that a former union is beyond repair.

From the biblical standpoint, then, no essential purpose is served by requiring the life of singleness after divorce, and only intransigent asceticism would insist on it. The tragic results of a break-up are only prolonged and intensified by submitting to a monastic rule that none of the Bible spokesmen require. The tag ends of a divorce need all the help they can get. The biblical principles free such a bereft partner to seek a godly mate and responsible parent for the children, thus enabling the healing process to take place in a reconstructed home.

4. *Does living together constitute marriage?* Cohabitation or common-law marriages have multiplied in recent years for various reasons. Such an arrangement allows for physical companionship and sexual gratification without the traditional responsibilities attached. Some even realize tax benefits from it. Being a "throw-away" relationship, it seduces by its temporary nature and many are allured by it. When such a couple become believers and desire to find God's will for their lives, how should they regard their relation to each other? Are they married, or what is their status? Since Paul says that, "the one who joins himself to a harlot is one body with her" (1 Cor. 6:16 NASB), does such a couple's physical union constitute marriage?

We should first recall what makes a marriage. It is constituted by the exchange of vows, the legal endorsement of society, and the consummation act of physical union. Cohabiting in sexual relations is performing the marriage act in God's eyes, but it is not endorsed by society nor cemented by a public commitment of faithfulness to each other. Without this personal exchange of vows and a proper recognition by society, the relation is only a physical counterfeit of true marriage. It is a form of "living in adultery." Personal commitment to each other is necessary to weld them together spiritually and psychologically, and a legal pronouncement is necessary to relate to society and to conform to the laws of the land.

What then should such a couple do to get their marital house in order for God to bless? After confessing their sins, they should make a solemn commitment of faithfulness to each other and comply with the legal statutes for marriage. If they already have children, they might regard their marriage as beginning at the time they started living together to relieve any future embarrassments for the children. Many states allow this and it is true to the physical aspects of the marriage.

All three of these elements are essential to a proper marriage relationship to help promote its permanency. They give the marriage stability by relieving the fears and insecurity of a mere convenience union that may terminate at any time. True marriage is a relationship that relates to God and society as well as to the couple themselves. It is bonded by a solid personal commitment to each other and is made legitimate by the legal endorsement of society. This is the marital union God blesses.

5. *How to correct a polygamous union.* On occasion missionaries face the difficult problem of counseling a newly saved man with several wives. Perhaps he has made commitments to all of them and all are recognized as his wives. Inasmuch as the Old Testament portrays many such plural-wife relations, would it be wrong for a believer to continue to maintain such a "harem"? What biblical counsel might be given to such a situation to insure God's blessing on the home?

Let me first observe that it is not the business of a missionary, pastor, or counselor to "tell" counselees what to do (although psychiatrists often have to deal with neurotics and psychotics in this way). Normally, it is better for the individuals themselves to make their own decisions. This helps them to think through their problems more thoroughly, places the responsibility on them personally, and gives them more incentive to follow through on the decisions made. The counselor's responsibilities are to help them see all the issues in the clearest light and to give them a proper basis for action. In discussing the propriety of marital decisions, they should help them see the biblical principles involved.

Although polygamy was engaged in during the Old Testament period, it is strongly urged against in the New Testament. The practice of polygamy actually began in the wicked line of Cain and was engaged in by the godly when they were out of God's will. It almost always brought dissension in the home, as seen in the lives of Abraham, Jacob, and David. In determining our ethical and moral standards today, however, our recourse must be to the full revelation of the New Testament, not the incomplete revelation of the Old. In the New Testament, we are instructed that believers are to have a "one-wife" or "one-husband" character. Even the Old Testament prophet Malachi declared this as essential to produce a godly line. Paul declared that leaders of the church are to exemplify this quality for the flock to follow. The fact that Christ is taking the whole church as His bride is not a contradiction of this principle. The church in those passages (Eph. 5:22-32; Rev. 19:7) is seen as a single "wife" or "bride" of Christ, not a flock of wives. It is an analogy which points up His headship and close relation to each of us, not an allegory to be interpreted in all its parts. The God-ordained example of proper marriage was given in Eden where God joined one man and one woman together in marital union. And this is the union He has chosen to bless.

What recourse then does a polygamist who is saved

have in establishing himself and his family in the will of God? After discussing with his wives the Bible's teaching on proper marriage, the best probably resolution would be to recognize the first one married as his proper wife. He should still assume responsibility for the others, however, as far as support is concerned. As each of the additional wives marries another, that responsibility would end. In such an arrangement, there would doubtless be complications concerning children and their support which would have to be worked out, but the framework of biblical principles would be set up. With that I believe God would give grace and an amicable solution to the marital entanglement.

6. *The plight of a partner confined to a nursing home.* The problems of the aged in matrimony sometimes equal those of the young. The loss of physical attractions and abilities in the waning years can be most frustrating. A woman just past middle age became ill and was confined to a nursing home. Her husband attended her quite faithfully, but their physical relations were fairly sundered. As her decline continued, she changed psychologically and her affections, once very warm, were almost gone. In the long vigil the husband, yet virile, became enamored with a friend and wondered about the propriety of divorce and remarriage to the new companion, while yet supporting his former wife. Inasmuch as the marital relation was practically dead and their affections seemingly gone, he pondered whether there was any point in waiting for death to part them.

While such a divorce and remarriage might seem reasonable and justified by the newly enamored couple, there would be no biblical ground for such an action. The reasons would be selfish. As the marriage vows properly read, he is to "love, honor, and keep her, in illness and in health; and forsaking all others you will keep faithfully unto her,

117

so long as you both shall live." When one partner is no longer able to show affection, for whatever physical or psychological reasons, that affection is often needed the most. The difficulties it entails, whether recognized or not, may offer some of the greatest values to both parties. The bed-ridden wife would not be the only loser. For the husband to desert his life companion maritally in this hour of need would damage his own self-worth, as well as his character in the eyes of others. Also His new mate would have good reason to question his future faithfulness to her. One who cannot stand true in times of stress and trials is not genuinely worthy of anyone's trust. On both biblical and human grounds, such a desertion (though not a physical desertion) would amount to sheer selfishness and unfaithfulness when that trust is needed most.

7. *When is it proper to remarry a divorced partner?* Remarriage to one's previous mate is not uncommon. Generally such a remarriage is the only proper course in pursuing God's will, but at times it may be improper. An unsaved couple was divorced and the wife then married another man. Later she divorced her second husband and had aspirations again for her first husband. He was yet unmarried. In the meantime, however, he had become a Christian and was concerned about doing God's will. The question then arose as to whether he had an obligation to remarry her with a view to leading her to faith in Christ and establishing a Christian home.

Several factors indicate that such a remarriage would be wrong. In the eyes of God she was still married to her second husband, though that marriage had begun with adultery. For the first husband to remarry her would then become a second act of adultery. Even the law of Moses forbade such a second union, calling it an abomination to marry back and forth. Second, he would be marrying an unbeliever. Such action hardly carries with it the promise of God's blessing and would likely create even greater tension in the home than they had had before. Third, it would be foolhardy indeed to marry one who had been twice divorced and had never come to repentance before God. The third time is not necessarily a charm for one who has established a pattern of unfaithfulness and incompatibility. Biblically speaking, such a re-union has no proper warrant.

Let's assume, however, that both were believers, though out of God's will through this entanglement. That would eliminate the problem of marrying an unbeliever with its dangers. Would such a remarriage be wise and proper, one of the divorced partners having been married and divorced a second time, since their divorce took place? Again, the biblical principles suggest that this would be wrong, inasmuch as she was still married to her second husband in the eyes of God. Her responsibility was to become reconciled to her second husband, not to the first one.

This situation was faced by another couple with some additional wrinkles. Some years ago they had been married and divorced, and later one of them was married and divorced a second time. In the meantime, however, this original couple had both been saved individually and also her second husband had remarried someone else. That, of course, eliminates the previous problem of a believer presuming to marry an unbeliever. It would also be free from the charge of adultery, inasmuch as the second husband would have already dissolved their marriage by his remarriage. Both were not believers and all previous marriage relations were dissolved. Would this remarriage then be proper?

In terms of New Testament instruction, it appears to pass most of the tests of propriety, some by default. Recalling the Mosaic injunction, however, it might yet consti-

an abomination in God's eyes because of the intervening marriage. Their pattern of wife-swapping activities would be after the fashion of the world and thus an abomination to God. Perhaps the one mitigating factor might be that they were saved following the marital disasters and were now dedicated to God and determined to do His will. That would be an appeal to the spirit of the Law rather than the letter in a difficult mix of scrambled ingredients. Such a life change might give the entanglement a new character and introduce a new potential for glorifying God in marital success.

8. *When is desertion proper grounds for divorce and remarriage?* A couple was separated but without a legal divorce. He simply left town and she was left with the children and the responsibilities of the home. After a period of time she was concerned to know what her responsibility was toward him and what her biblical rights were concerning divorce and possible remarriage.

This problem could be stated with many variations, for, as previously noted, desertions are nearly as numerous as legal divorces. In some ways such separations are more devastating because of their suddenness and the uncertainty and the deserter's failure to make proper provisions for those left. What biblical principles relate to such bereft partners with respect to divorce and remarriage and their responsibility to care for the family?

We note first that Paul's counsel in 1 Corinthians 7 was that couples should not separate, and if one should leave, their one goal should be reconciliation. He recognized, however, that a willful partner might leave, and under those conditions he made no demands that the union be continued. Such a couple Paul described as "unmarried" (*agamos*, 1 Cor. 7:11). He appears to have assumed divorce in that case. The question is whether he also allowed remarriage by the partner that had been deserted. That he did not sanction such remarriage by the deserter is obvious, but what about the one left? Jesus' counsel was that marrying another after divorce constitutes adultery, except where sexual immorality has taken place. If we then assume the harmony of Jesus and Paul in this instruction, it is evident that Paul's desertion is not another ground for remarriage, but an elucidation of the exception Jesus expressed. Together they emphasized that sexual unfaithfulness is the one proper ground for remarriage, and, short of that, reconciliation is to be sought as long as there is hope.

The conclusion then is that desertion alone is not a proper ground for divorce and remarriage. Reconciliation should first be sought. If, however, adulterous relations have also accompanied the desertion, the circumstance is then changed and the deserted partner is free to divorce and remarry in God's will. But what about the partner who is left without any knowledge of the whereabouts or activities of the deserting partner? Is such to remain in that state of uncertainty and emptiness for life? It is usually conceded that if a desertion continues for a year or more, the marriage should be regarded as terminated, assuming the partner's unfaithfulness to the marriage covenant. In light of Jesus' assumption of remarriage after divorce and Paul's reference only to restrictions for the deserter, I think such a concession appropriate. The Jewish bethrothal period of waiting was also one year. Except in unusual circumstances, the period of a year would certainly show the deserter's unfaithfulness to the marriage vows and one can only assume sexual unfaithfulness as well. Though some would argue for a shorter time period, one's future uncertainty would be better allayed by persevering for at least a year to test the deserter's intentions of fulfilling the marriage vows. Such a period of desertion is generally conceded to indicate a dissolution of the marriage.

9. *Should a partner tolerate physical cruelty?* Although I do not refer to a specific case, the question is sometimes asked as to whether a Christian should stay with a mate who abuses him/her physically. This is somewhat the opposite of the previous problem where the partner deserted. With violence in society abounding, cruelty in marriage also abounds. A recent social survey of selected homes revealed such to be a problem in nearly half of these homes which were randomly picked throughout America. How submissive should a Christian be to such treatment?

Paul's instruction in 1 Corinthians 7 appears to grant the possibility that a wife might properly leave her husband in extreme situations. If she does, the apostle declares, she is to remain unmarried (1 Cor. 7:11). He later commands that the desertion of an unbeliever be accepted in the interest of preserving peace (1 Cor. 7:15). Peter likewise charged that husbands should live with honor toward their wives as the "weaker vessels," treating them as fellow-heirs of the grace of life" (1 Peter 3:7 NASB).

Though the Bible does not specifically address the problem, I do not believe that a wife should long continue a relationship in which she is made to suffer physical brutality. Separation for religious reasons or for mere disagreements is not allowed, but cruelty is another matter. To tolerate it is to condone it. Paul's injunction that the wife be submissive was not meant to imply that she should meekly accept violence. He did not mean that she should tolerate what God abhors. It is the part of prudence for a wife to withdraw from such a situation as best she can in the interest of all parties involved. Such a withdrawal, of course, is easier said than done, but the biblical principles would hardly deny its propriety. As with a partner who is sexually unfaithful, such an intemperate partner needs to be shocked into a realization of the consequence of his

122

actions, and leaving him "high and dry" to ponder those consequences is better therapy than allowing it to continue. The purpose of such a withdrawal, of course, should be reconciliation, and a reassurance of love and faithfulness might well be required by the wife to resume those relations. God has called us to marital peace, and condoning cruelty does not promote such peace.

10. *Should a divorced person be allowed to serve as a deacon or deaconess?* A man applied for membership in a certain church and was told that he could join, but neither he nor his wife could teach or serve in any leadership position. He had been married and divorced a number of years earlier, prior to his conversion, and that placed him in a special non-leadership category in the church. This has been the traditional position of many churches based on the belief that Paul required elders and deacons to have had a perfect marital history in his admonition that they be the "husband of one wife" (1 Tim. 3:2, 12; Titus 1:6).

As noted on pages 78–89 and 98–101, we believe this view to be based on a misunderstanding of the phrase it grounds itself on. Paul's concern in giving the leadership qualifications was not to insist on their having had a perfect history but that they have an honorable and praiseworthy present character. All the qualifications in these passages reflect this concern for choosing leaders with moral and spiritual maturity. In this light, the "one-wife" man qualification is better understood in terms of marital stability, as we noted in earlier chapters. The church is to carefully scrutinize a candidate's character, rather than merely his legal credentials. This does not play down the sin of divorce and remarriage, for that enters into an evaluation of his character. But neither does it make a marital tragedy, regardless of how it occurred, to be an unpardonable sin as far as Christian service is concerned. It does not inflate that sin to a level that is more heinous than murder, rape, and other sins which are supposedly subject to pardon and erase for Christian service.

The question of divorced people serving in leadership roles then depends on their spiritual maturity and growth since the break-up occurred. If the lessons have been learned and applied and a solid character of marital stability has been demonstrated, then there is no biblical basis for restricting such a person in his service for Christ in the church. To do so would be a loss for both the church and the individuals involved. The period of recovery and reestablishment, of course, would be different for different people and situations. It would depend on the individual's repentance, acknowledgment of error, and the evidence of a new commitment and reliance on God. Some time would necessarily be required for this process, but the person's leadership gifts and service should not be aborted permanently simply because the church cannot forgive the sin.

11. *What about the guilty party?* A man came to my office with a different kind of problem. He was the "villain," rather than the "victim." He had been unfaithful to his wife and she had divorced him and was now married to another man. With no possibility of reconciliation with her and with a new commitment to do God's will, what was his status with regard to remarriage and what were his prospects concerning Christian service?

In confronting marital problems, we usually hear from the "innocent" party, but not nearly so often from the so-called "guilty." This may reflect a reluctance of people to admit their guilt, of course, but it may also suggest some of the hopelessness of the guilty who feel unworthy to seek counsel, sympathy, and restoration. By the terms innocent and guilty we refer to the sin of illicit sex, not suggesting that the faults are necessarily all one-sided. The church has traditionally had little time or sympathy for this guilty party, and its counseling manuals reflect this attitude.

What does the Bible require of such a person? Can he or she remarry in God's will? Can they hope to develop their character and spiritual gifts with a view to serving in some leadership roles in the church? Or, is this sin unpardonable in these respects?

Although the Bible does not propound a "no-fault" policy on divorce, it does treat both parties of a break-up similarly in the process of restoration. It is not that the guilty is exonerated with a wave of the hand and will not have to pay dearly for causing the marital break-up. That payment will certainly be exacted in God's sovereign way. But the way back to God's will and blessing is open to all, the innocent and guilty alike. The Lord doesn't distinguish between them as far as offering forgiveness is concerned. Where there is true repentance and confession, and proper restitution is made, God's forgiveness and grace are fully given.

Therefore, the guilty party would have the same privileges as the innocent following the process of restoration. When a former partner is remarried, there is little point in requiring the guilty one to remain unmarried, unless it be to fulfill some punitive rule. Not only would it be unrealistic to expect, it would serve no biblical purpose, inasmuch as the former marriage would be completely dissolved. Paul taught that an unmarried person with sexual passions should get married, and the Lord Himself declared in Eden that "It is not good that the man (or woman) should be alone" (Gen. 2:18). Thus, to require such a person to remain unmarried would contradict rather than comply with biblical principles.

The same might also apply to their Christian service. Christian service is not restricted to those with perfect histories, whether marital or otherwise. It is for those who have drunk deeply of the grace of God and applied that grace and discipline to their lives to develop their character and spiritual gifts for His glory. If one has been guilty of marital unfaithfulness, a dangerous trait of character is obviously indicated. Such an act of passions tends to repeat itself. But to insist that this is always so is to deny the power of God's grace in one's life. It is to deny the transforming power of the gospel. While the church is to carefully evaluate the lives of its leaders, it is not to disdain God's grace in its ability to salvage sinners, even the guilty party in a marriage break-up.

12. *Should parents intervene to prevent "wrong" marriages by their children?* This question arises out of a variety of situations. It may relate to early teen-age romances, live-in or pregnancy situations, or to unfortunate matches contemplated by children who are beyond the age of parental supervision. At whatever age or stage, the prospects of having one's children unequally joined with ungodly or undesirable mates is a jolting experience. And ironically, it happens even to those who seem to be committed Christians. What counsel does the Bible give for such a dilemma?

We must start with the fundamental biblical principle that a believer should not marry an unbeliever. To violate this is to invite continual strife and probably compromise in spiritual principles. True, such a mismatch may not be entirely lost, but it starts with two strikes against it. Myriads of such cases testify to the despair of well-intentioned believers who were deluded into thinking they could evangelize their partners in the aftermath. The cruel fact is that it rarely works that way. But the time to give this instruction is not after the romance has started and their natural attractions have bonded. That is years too late. Once the love bug bites or the romantic flame is lit, it is difficult to snuff out, even with biblical principles and clarion warnings. Emotions tend to override rational principles. This, of course, is why it is always dangerous for

Christian young people to date unbelievers. A candle close to the flame easily catches fire.

When Christian parents are suddenly faced with this dilemma, they also become torn between emotions and reason. Armed with a knowledge of how wrong the union would be, they often tend to react with shock, shame, and anger. This overreaction breeds further hostility and defiance by the young people which destroys good rapport for parental counsel in the days ahead. How then should Christian parents respond to salvage such a situation?

Rather than scolding or arguing, their primary recourse should be prayer. If a son or daughter makes such a decision against parental wishes, they are probably prepared with arguments to defend it. At the engagement point they are usually ready to fend off all comers against their lover, parents included. Here it is well to remember that "A gentle answer turns away wrath, but a harsh word stirs up anger" (Prov. 15:1 NASB). A firm statement of disapproval should certainly be given, emphasizing the disharmony and strife that such a mismatch will bring (2 Cor. 6:14). The stress should be on the young people's happiness, not on the parents' outrage. It should be done in gentleness and love, not in anger. The lines of communication must be kept open so that further guidance can be received. Fervent prayer should then be made that the Lord will intervene in His own sovereign way to bring about the salvation of the unsaved lover or the break-up of the engagement. Such a prayer can be prayed with full assurance that one of these is God's will. The parent should then trust God to accomplish one or the other through events leading up to the wedding day, hopefully through pastoral counseling. It can be a growing though traumatic experience, in which the parent learns to trust God through new commitment and believing prayer.

It is well to remember that at this point mere parental

control or prohibition is futile. The need for parental consent to marry is often more legal than actual. If a decision is forced upon the young people, they easily find ways to enforce their own, sometimes with embarrassing consequences. They feel mature, whether they are or not, and usually resent any suggestions to the contrary. Therefore, they must be reminded that the decision is theirs, not merely one forced on them by their parents. The Lord can use other roadblocks to deter them en route to the altar. A faithful pastor, for instance, will remind them that he has no biblical right to officiate at such a ceremony, giving them further cause to ponder. Rather than pulling the responsibility away from them by parental edict, the parents should place it firmly on them with assurances of their great love and concern for them as they evaluate the decision.

In spite of everything, however, the mismatched couple may go through with the marriage, principles and prayer notwithstanding. Their decision then must be accepted by the parents and it is futile for them to fight it. To do so often leads to worse consequences. The parents of a girl who was pregnant wondered how they could properly give their daughter away to an unsaved man with whom she had been living. They had refused them permission to marry and were even now reluctant. They needed to face the obvious fact that the young couple were already joined and to deny it now was pure fantasy. To force them to separate would have been the greater error. The parents' responsibility at that point was to help them stabilize the union by their getting a marriage license and exchanging vows of faithfulness to each other. A pastor faced with this problem, I believe, should have no qualms about performing the ceremony, for the marriage was already consummated. His officially "tying the knot" would not be joining them in marriage so much as it would be helping them salvage a bad start in their journey on a difficult road. It would also build a bridge for future counsel. A couple in these circumstances needs positive help, not rejection and scorn. Redemptive forces must be called into play.

This is true of all marriages that are wrongfully made, whether in rebellion or ignorance. When the decision is made and insisted on, it has to be accepted, even though it is contrary to scriptural wisdom. A redemptive strategy then has to be employed by the parents and concerned Christian friends. The parents' marital plan "A" for their son or daughter may have to be substituted with a redemptive plan "B." This is not done by demeaning the union as second-rate, but by building the best relations possible and showing Christian concern. Though God does not normally work this way, His grace is not limited to the normal. Redemptive marriages all around us remind us that we should not underestimate God's redemptive grace, even in the marital arena.

Appendix

The Meaning of Jesus' Exception for Divorce

Much of the controversy as to the Bible's view of divorce and remarriage centers on two statements by Jesus. These are given in Matthew 5:32 and 19:9 where He includes an exception to the sin of divorce. These exception clauses are most significant, inasmuch as all the other New Testament references to divorce and remarriage hinge on this initial instruction by the Lord. It is therefore essential that we grasp the significance of these brief exception clauses.

The problem involved in these clauses is really threefold: 1) Why are these exceptions recorded by Matthew, but not by Mark or Luke? 2) What did Jesus mean by the term "fornication"? 3) Did this exception also allow the right to remarry? Simply stated, it is the problem of how to harmonize the passages that speak of the permanence of marriage with those that allow for divorce. The apparent contradictions in these statements by Jesus have long troubled the church, and the struggle is not less intense in our day. We owe the problem our serious consideration if we are to get the Bible's balanced view on the subject. Various solutions have been offered of which we shall note the most prominent.

Why Matthew Alone Records the Exceptions.

The first question concerns the reasons why Jesus' exceptions were given by Matthew, but not by the other Gospel writers. A popular solution has been to suggest that the exception clauses recorded by Matthew were not the genuine words of Jesus, but were added by an early scribe of the church. The answer to this seeming discrepancy then is to simply delete the exception clauses by Matthew as spurious and disregard them. This scissors treatment would be a handy way of disposing of a thorny problem, but it has no objective base. As previously noted (p. 50), the textual support for these passages is very strong. Lack of apparent harmony is no ground for dismissing a difficult passage as being spurious. That very difficulty, in fact, supports its genuineness, for later scribes tended to smooth out difficulties, not to introduce them. It is our responsibility to discern the meaning of the texts as we have them, not to judge their accuracy by whether we understand them. As far as the genuineness of these texts is concerned (Matt. 5:32; 19:9; Mark 10:11, 12; and Luke 16:18), we can rest assured that they all have strong textual support.

The question then remains as to why Matthew recorded the exception but not the others. As with many other omissions by various Gospels, the reason lies in the individual purpose of each. Matthew, for instance, omitted nearly the whole "Travelogue" of Luke 9:51 to 18:17; Mark omitted all of Matthew's Sermon on the Mount; and John omitted much of the material recorded by the other Gospels. The obvious reason is that each writer had a specific purpose in writing and was guided by the Holy Spirit in the selection of materials to fulfill that purpose. This purpose-principle helps us to understand why Matthew included the exception clause, though Mark and Luke did not.

The reasons for the omissions by Mark and Luke are different, however, and it will help to review each. In Matthew 19 and Mark 10, the incident referred to is the same but the responses by Jesus are different. The reason is that He responded to two different groups. On that occasion, Jesus was across the Jordan and was confronted first by the Pharisees in an outside assembly and later by the disciples in a house (Mark 10:10). Matthew recorded His reply to the Pharisees who had asked the question, and Mark recorded His later summary statement to the disciples. The fuller statement to the Pharisees was in response to their mischievous query as to what might be legitimate grounds for divorce. To them He gave a clarification based on the Old Testament which included the exception clause. Having given this explanation to the general audience outside, the Lord did not repeat it to the disciples in the house. To them He simply restated His basic point of the intended permanence of marriage and the tragedy of its being broken. Thus the two statements recorded by Matthew and Mark are not different versions of the same statement, as if Mark only summarized the statement by Matthew. They are rather two different declarations to two different groups, one giving the principle of permanent marriage with one divinely recognized exception, and the other simply restating the basic principle.

In Luke's account, however, the setting is different and the emphasis of the conversation is entirely different (Luke 16:18). Jesus was here confronted by another group of Pharisees who derided Him for His low view of worldly riches. As they scoffed, He declared them to be worshipers of mammon while pretending to be worshipers of God. He reminded them that God looks at the heart, and will hold them accountable for every "stroke of a letter of the Law" (vv. 15, 17, NASB). To impress this truth even deeper into their calloused consciences, Jesus then rehearsed to them

God's intention for them to have permanent marriages, a principle often violated by those of the "school of Hillel." In so doing, Jesus made no mention of the exception, for that was not in question at this time. His statement here was simply a reminder of the general principle to further rebuke their self-justifying practice of living by their passions.

The point to be noted is that the three Gospels are not contradictory but supplementary in these statements. They record faithfully three different statements by Jesus on the subject of marriage and the danger of adultery. All the details supplied by the three Gospels are important, and it is folly to reject any of them simply because they are recorded by only one writer. To treat the rest of the Gospel details in that way would produce utter chaos. We don't reject John 3:16 on the basis of its omission by Matthew, Mark, and Luke. Likewise, we have no ground for deleting this exception clause which is twice given by Matthew, except it be pious or creedal prejudice. Both the text and context strongly support its authenticity.

The Meaning of "Fornication" in the Exception Clause.

Having established its genuineness, we then ask what it means. What specifically did Jesus mean by the term "fornication" (Porneia)? That it was some kind of sexual aberration which was inimical to the marriage relation is, of course, generally agreed. The specific kind of sexual sin, however, has been the point of some controversy. Let's review several popular views that are held today and then elucidate what appears to be the most biblically accurate and consistent meaning of the word.

The consanguineous view. There are those who interpret the Lord's use of "porneia" in Matthew 5:32 and 19:19 as a reference to the Mosaic prohibition against marriage to blood relatives (Lev. 18:6-18). Since Jesus' audience was primarily Jewish, His reference could be to this sin. Paul, also, used the word "porneia" in this sense in 1 Corinthians 5:1, which suggests its recognition also by Gentile Christians.

This interpretation, however, would restrict Jesus' exception of fornication to those who have married blood relatives and would deny its application to other forms of fornication. Those taking this view also generally see it as limited to the Jews of Jesus' time who were under the Mosaic legislation. The practical effect of this view then is to deny the application of the exception clause to our day in any way. It restricts it to a Jewish problem of Jesus' time alone.

The grammatical problem with this restricted view is that the word *porneia* has a much broader usage throughout the Bible. It is used twenty-six times in the New Testament with reference to all kinds of sexual immorality. The only direct reference to consanguineous marriage is 1 Corinthians 5:1. Furthermore, the word is used in the Greek translation of the Old Testament (LXX) many times as a translation of the Hebrew term *zanah*, which meant "playing the harlot" (Gen. 38:24; Jer. 3:1; Ezek. 16:28; Hos. 3:3, etc.). This version, by the way, was the Greek Bible of Jesus' time. And Jesus Himself used the word *porneia* in a variety of ways. On the other hand, this restricted meaning of "marriage to blood relatives" was not a common one, for the sin was most extraordinary. In Paul's only use of it in this way in 1 Corinthians 5:1, he denounced the sin as a horrible instance of licentiousness which was unheard of even among the Gentiles. It was a case in which the libertine spirit of Corinth had grossly distorted the grace of God. Likewise, there is no evidence that the Jews of Jesus' time allowed this sin among them which was so clearly denounced by Moses. John's condemnation of Herod the heathen king for this offense only shows how heinous and

135

extraordinary it was. Thus, there is very little grammatical or contextual evidence that Jesus referred to this sin of living with blood relatives in His use of the term *porneia*. Though that sin is included, it is extremely questionable that that was Jesus' primary point in the exception clause.

The view that porneia means unfaithfulness during betrothal. Another view that is being popularized today is that Jesus used the term *porneia* to refer to unfaithfulness during a couple's betrothal period, prior to actual marriage. This is postulated on the ground that there is a difference between fornication (*porneia*) and adultery (*moicheia*). The case of Joseph considering divorce from Mary before their marriage is often suggested as an example of such a sin (although Mary, of course, was not guilty of it). Although the word *porneia* is not actually used in that passage (Matt. 1:18-19), the concept of divorce before marriage is proposed. The point is that the betrothal agreement was so binding for the Jews that a divorce was required to break it. However, since we do not carry on that Jewish custom in our society, the exception of fornication can have no relevance for us today. It supposedly had a rare application to the time of Jesus only.

This view is admittedly another good cultural way of disposing of the exception clause for our day. Intriguing though it may be, and pious though its adherents, the interpretation has several serious defects. It is first to be noted that the word *porneia* is never used anywhere in the New Testament to describe the sin of illicit relations during betrothal. It could, but it isn't. Second, there is nothing in the immediate contexts of Matthew to suggest such a restrictive use of the term. No restriction of its wider usage is even suggested. Finally, that interpretation would not fit the logic of Jesus' statement in either of the exception clauses. Let's notice how illogical it would be in either of the passages by stating the principle Jesus enunciated (by this interpretation) without the exception. In Matthew 5:32, He would be saying that "everyone who divorces his wife (or betrothed) makes her commit adultery." In Matthew 19:9, He would be saying that "whoever divorces his wife (or betrothed) and marries another commits adultery." In other words, if Joseph had divorced Mary during their betrothal period, both he and she would have committed adultery, according to this view. To break an engagement would constitute adultery. Such an interpretation then would introduce a new definition of adultery which is never suggested in the Bible. Or, it would suggest that the Jews normally had sexual relations before marriage during the betrothal period, an unthinkable supposition.

It is thus evident that this view of fornication has no biblical support in either the grammar or contexts. It introduces a restriction on Jesus' words which is both unbiblical and illogical in the statements Jesus made. Well-intentioned though the view may be, it is completely contrived and finds its basis on other creedal presuppositions. The reason Jesus used the term "fornication" rather than "adultery" in this clause is certainly significant, but that purpose was much broader, as we shall presently note.

The view that porneia means marriage to Gentiles or heathen. A third prominent explanation is one that takes its support from the Old Testament books of Ezra and Nehemiah (Ezra 10:3, 11, 19; Neh. 13:23-30). In these passages the problem of heathen marriages and divorces was being dealt with by these postexilic leaders. Ezra and Nehemiah rebuked the many Jews who had married heathen wives, reminding them that such marriages often led their forefathers to idolatry. To correct this violation of the Mosaic law, they counseled the radical action of divorce. This was a case where divorce was in fact advised.

137

To properly understand these Old Testament divorces, however, it is necessary to note the similar action referred to in Malachi 2:10-17. In that passage, Malachi also reprimanded certain Jewish men for marrying heathen women and "dealing treacherously" with their Jewish wives, or the "wife of your youth" (Mal. 2:14, 15). These Jewish wives (whom they had married first) should have been their only wives, in line with God's plan for monogamous marriage (Mal. 2:15). To divorce such, Malachi declared, was something God hated. It constituted a trade-off of their older wives for new heathen ones, or the addition of heathen wives along with their first wife. With this situation of Malachi in mind, it is probable that Ezra and Nehemiah counseled separation on the same ground. The long counseling sessions that followed suggest a reconstruction of their family affairs. Marrying Gentile women after their purification was allowed by Moses, but divorcing a wife was not, except for sexual uncleanness (Deut. 21:10-13; 22:29; 24:1-4). It is doubtful that Ezra, the great law scholar, would counsel a deviation from Moses. It is more probable that these leaders counseled separation from heathen wives when the man involved was already married to a Jewish wife, a situation analogous to that of Abraham separating from Hagar.

With this in mind, it is extremely doubtful that Jesus' exception clauses suggested the propriety of divorcing heathen wives. Marriage to Gentiles was not considered to be fornication, as such. To see it as allowing divorce from heathen wives would contradict Moses and result in utter chaos, whether applied to Jesus' time or to our own. That was specifically what Paul warned against in 1 Corinthians 7:10. That kind of divorce, by the way, is very similar to the allowance made by the Roman Catholic concept of nullity as traditionally applied. Even they are currently questioning the concept as a rationalization for convenience.

It will be observed that the three views of fornication or *porneia* just examined have one thing in common: they all relegate the exception clause primarily to the Jewish culture of Jesus' time. Each one seizes upon a different but quite restrictive interpretation of *porneia* to invalidate Jesus' exception clause for today. In so doing, they reduce the Lord's counsel on divorce and remarriage in the three Gospels to one basic proposition. That is that there is no valid grounds for divorce today in the eyes of God—under any circumstances. Marriage is permanent or indissoluble and no kind or amount of sexual sins can sever that bond. This view, of course, has long been that of the Catholic Church, although they authenticate it on other grounds and qualify it in other ways. Even Catholic scholars are arising to question this indissolubility in the light of the New Testament and early church fathers. Ideal though this indissoluble view may be, we believe it violates the explicit words of Jesus and builds on pious idealism rather than on biblical truth.

The view that porneia includes all extramarital sex relations. The remaining alternative to which we are driven suffers from the fact that it is the most obvious. In both the New Testament and the Septuagint the term *porneia* is almost universally used in the sense of "harlotry of any kind." Arndt and Gingrich in their *Lexicon of the New Testament* define it as "every kind of unlawful sexual intercourse" (p. 699). This was also how the Reformers understood the exception clauses in Matthew, as they led the return from church dogma to biblical exegesis. They saw no biblical reason to reject either the text of the obvious meaning of the text for a far-fetched, rare, cultural explanation. Only foreign presuppositions would dictate otherwise.

139

We should note that the term "fornication" (*porneia*) is broader than the term "adultery" (*moicheia*). Whereas adultery concerns unfaithfulness of marriage partners, fornication includes all kinds of illicit sex, both in and out of the marriage relation. The question then arises as to why Jesus used the term porneia rather than moicheia, inasmuch as His exception related to unfaithfulness by marriage partners. Why didn't He use the term adultery in both instances to avoid the confusion? The obvious reason is in the context. Jesus used the broader term to emphasize God's insistence on moral purity and to rebuke the moral laxity of many leaders who kept the letter of the Law but not the spirit. By using this broader term, the Lord closed any loopholes for those who saw adultery as only the sin of having relations with another man's wife (Lev. 20:10). In so doing, He emphasized God's judgment on all kinds of extramarital sex and declared the devastating effect such activity has on a marriage.

What then was Jesus' point in making fornication an exception to the rule that divorce becomes adultery? His point was that such fornication would have already constituted the heinous sin of adultery, making de facto divorce already in effect. The marriage vow of sexual faithfulness would be already severed by that fornication, and the union would be a living lie. Paul likewise declared that "the one who joins himself to a harlot is one body with her" (1 Cor. 6:16 NASB). This he confirmed by a quote from Moses that such a sexual union constitutes marriage. The marriage it constitutes is an illicit one to be sure, but it breaks the "one-flesh" union of the previous marriage, leaving it in a shambles. It does not mean that it cannot be repaired, but that the intimate bond has been broken.

With these clarifications, let's put together the four statements of Jesus on divorce as recorded by Matthew, Mark, and Luke.

Except where sexual infidelity has already occurred, any man or woman who obtains a divorce commits adultery (in view of his or her subsequent remarriage) and furthermore causes his or her spouse and future mate to commit adultery as well. Where infidelity has been the cause, however, that divorce would not constitute adultery, inasmuch as the union would have already been broken in its most vital relation.

His point was that although God joins a marrying couple together for a permanent union, that relation can be broken by their hardness of heart in violating their commitment to sexual faithfulness. Such faithfulness between partners is absolutely essential to a proper marriage relation.

Conclusion. This view of the sin of fornication is admittedly a most stringent one. It reveals Jesus' total intolerance of sexual promiscuity whether in or out of the marriage relation. The minimal requirement for marriage is such faithfulness. As with all sin, Jesus allowed no mitigation of judgment for sexual infidelity in marriage in terms of immediate consequences. Although forgiveness is always available through repentance and restitution, the physical consequences of sin are not alleviated. To commit murder is to reap the judgment of death, and believers are not exempt. To steal is to invite wrath. And to commit adultery is to reap a broken marriage. Even Paul the apostle of grace confirmed this consequence of moral prostitution. Though God hates divorce, He detests and abominates moral promiscuity even more.

It is true that there are those who might rationalize these words of Jesus as an easy way out of a bad marriage relation. One can gain scriptural grounds for divorce by "simply having an affair." Such thinking, however, misses the point Jesus was making. It would be like saying that the way to avoid death is to commit suicide. Jesus' point was that both fornication and adultery are viewed by God as deserving the greatest judgment. The judgment for adultery in the Old Testament was the same as for murder, blasphemy, and idolatry. Far from providing loopholes for easy divorce or suggesting that one sin compensates for another, the Lord thundered out the great displeasure of God on all sexual promiscuity. Though He provides mercy and grace to all who are truly repentant, He never pares down the consequences of playing fast and loose with God's demands for moral purity. Thus these exception clauses speak of both His unbending judgment and His restorative grace for those who will recognize the tragedy and respond in obedience to His redemptive grace.

The Right to Remarry in the Exception Clause

Granting that Jesus' exception clause allows the right to divorce when unfaithfulness occurs, does that right also carry with it the right to remarry? As noted in chapter 5, we believe that it does when reconciliation is no longer possible. Some apparent contradictions, however, need resolving. Let's first establish what Jesus said on the subject and then examine two seemingly contradictory statements by the Apostle Paul.

Jesus' reference to remarriage. In His first exception clause (Matt. 5:32), Jesus addressed Himself primarily to divorce, not remarriage. In this statement, however, He did assume that the divorced wife would remarry. The man who divorces his wife, He said, "makes her commit adultery," and also makes the one marrying her to commit adultery. In other words, remarriage in that culture was not even questioned. Nor was it ever denied in the Old Testament. Without proper grounds, of course, the act of remarriage became an act of adultery. But by His assertion in the exception clause, Jesus showed remarriage to be free of the charge of adultery when the first union had been

142

broken by fornication. This did not reduce the sin of fornication, but declared its devastating effect in destroying a
marriage. Thus Jesus acknowledged that a second marriage might properly take place when a first one had been
broken by this illicit sin. As Jesus had just declared (Matt.
5:17), His view was not greatly different from Moses'
legislation, only identifying more specifically the "indecency" that constituted proper grounds for divorce. In this
first statement then, Jesus strongly implied that remarriage
would take place after divorce, amounting to adultery for
some, but not for others.

In the second exception clause (Matt. 19:9), however,
Jesus did speak of both divorce and remarriage. Without
the exception, these would constitute adultery. Although
He only implied it in Matthew 5, He directly stated it in
this passage. But again Jesus inserted the exception of
fornication which negates the proposition for those involved. Although some interpreters have related the exception only to divorce, both the logic and grammar require the involvement of both divorce and remarriage. To
quote John Murray, "In the syntax of the sentence as it
actually is, the meaning and relevance of the exceptive
clause cannot be maintained apart from its application to
the remarriage as well as to the putting away" (*Divorce*, p.
41). It might be noted that the exceptive clause and the
verb are in precisely the right place syntactically to emphasize this point. It is thus evident that on both occasions
Jesus acknowledged the possibility of remarriage after divorce and the propriety of it under certain circumstances.
Not that those circumstances require it, but that they allow
it as an option. Jesus acknowledged that what God has
joined together in marriage can be separated through sin,
and that is the whole thrust of His warning and instruction
in these passages.

   Paul's references to remarriage. Two statements by

Paul speak of the permanence of marriage and appear to contradict the exceptions made by Jesus. The first is Romans 7:2: "For the married woman is bound by law to her husband while he is living; but if her husband dies, she is released from the law concerning the husband" (NASB). He then declares that remarriage to another while the former partner still lives amounts to adultery. How can such a clear statement be reconciled with the exception made by Jesus?

Again, it is essential to recognize the purpose of Paul's statement in order to understand its sweep. A text must be understood by its context. Paul was not giving instruction on marriage at this point, but simply using the general principles of marriage and remarriage as an analogy of the believer's union with Christ. As marriage is normally ended at the death of one spouse, so our death to the law system takes place as we are joined to Christ. His point is that Christ becomes our new husband or master for effective living. In saying this, however, Paul did not deny exceptions to the general rule. He began his argument by appealing to their knowledge of the Law (7:1), which obviously included Moses' legislation on divorce and remarriage. The analogy did not deal with exceptions but with the general principle in order to impress the spiritual truth. An analogy or parable is seldom meant to "walk on all four," but to make a single point. Controverting Jesus' exception to the general principle of permanent marriage was the furthest from Paul's thinking in this passage.

A similar statement is made by Paul in 1 Corinthians 7:39. Although his purpose is a bit different in this passage, his reference to the general principle of permanent marriage is similar. In this chapter he had already given some needed counsel on marriage, when to marry and when not to. His final advice to them seemed to favor the single state, perhaps because of "some distress" that was

144

upon them. Under such situations of stress, he declared, it is foolhardy to marry. To emphasize the point of going slow in "jumping into marriage," Paul reminded them that marriage is for life. He had no need of bringing up the exception noted by Jesus, for that was beside the point. He had already acknowledged that release from a spouse was conceivable under certain circumstances (vv. 11, 15, 27), but those exceptions were not relevant at this time. As in all literature, the Bible often states general principles for different purposes without listing the exceptions which may be noted elsewhere.

It is evident then that there are no contradictions between the marriage counsel of Moses, Jesus, and Paul. Seeming contradictions only appear when statements are taken out of their contexts and we fail to recognize that each one wrote or spoke in full recognition of what was previously given. Jesus acknowledged His accord with Moses, and Paul constantly appealed to the counsel of Jesus. All of them emphasized the general principle of the permanence of marriage in this life, but all of them also acknowledged the possible disruptive effect of sin on a marriage. In the wake of such a tragedy, they allowed for a new union under proper circumstances, that the tragedy might be redeemed and God's purposes fulfilled in a redemptive setting. God's specialty is not only construction, but also reconstruction.

Subject Index

Subject Index

150

151

Scripture Index

Scripture Index

155